FATHER FORGIVE ME

Be extraordinary!
Enjoy the stories
[illegible] 2012

FATHER FORGIVE ME

KIM HAYNES JOHNSON

confessions of a
southern baptist
preacher's kid

Published by Tate Publishing & Enterprises, LLC
127 E. Trade Center Terrace | Mustang, Oklahoma 73064 USA
1.888.361.9473 | www.tatepublishing.com

Tate Publishing is committed to excellence in the publishing industry. The company reflects the philosophy established by the founders, based on Psalm 68:11,
"The Lord gave the word and great was the company of those who published it."

Cover design by Kristen Verser
Interior design by Nathan Harmony

Published in the United States of America

ISBN: 978-1-61862-940-1
1. Biography & Autobiography / Religious
2. Family & Relationships / Family Relationships
12.06.20

DEDICATION

This book is dedicated to Dr. and Mrs. Wilson Felix Haynes Jr., the best set of parents God ever gave anybody.

ACKNOWLEDGMENTS

I would like to thank my parents, Dr. and Mrs. Wilson Felix Haynes, Jr., for all of their love and support throughout my life. My brother, Ken, truly is a trooper; I owe him both gratitude and apologies for all that I have shared about his life. In an effort to protect church members—both the innocent and the guilty—I have changed the names of people and swapped church settings for some of the stories. All of the stories are true, and my deepest thanks go to all who participated in the stories I have shared. You have written my book in memories and moments that I only had to preserve with a pen.

A special thanks to those at Tate Publishing who believed in my book and helped with editing along the way—you are the best!

To PKs everywhere, thank you for upholding our reputation as extra-ordinary, extra-blessed people!

TABLE OF CONTENTS

THE NEW PK

"Preachers' kids are the worst!" This is an allegation we've heard all our lives. It was usually one of those heathen deacon's children hurling the accusation our way after we'd escaped blame for a problem we'd caused. Like livestock, PKs are branded for life. People know at first glance that we are trouble.

I'm still not sure whether the Blab-and-I'll-kill-you-myself threat understanding is innate in PKs, or whether it's a timed-release dose of hush that lasts until the next time the preacher tells the family, "Nothing you just saw or heard goes beyond these four walls." I tend to believe that it's inborn, though, because I've personally known so many gossiping preachers' wives. To my mother's credit, she was always the one doing the listening and reacting with mortified expressions, never the one spewing any of the venom.

There were times that I wondered—if I somehow survived childhood as a PK—whether I would ever turn out normal. But the PK I worried about the most was my brother. Ken is five years younger than I. Like most older siblings, I never let him forget he was the baby when we were younger, and he never lets me forget I am older than he is now that we're grown. My typical response is a less than gentle reminder that I wasn't the one whose hair started falling out before I was twenty-five. But that was the least of the problems my brother had growing up. Besides premature balding and having a preacher for a daddy, he was assigned me as a sister.

Our life together as siblings began as a standoff in the parsonage the day that my parents brought him home from the hospital. I agreed he was kind of cute, but I was a jealous child who began wondering if my parents could live better without me now that they had Ken. One morning, I decided to put them to the test. When no one was looking, I disappeared.

I remember hearing the muffled voices of my parents and others I didn't recognize. Doors opened and closed. A steady stream of footsteps flowed through the house. Miss Darby Hatley was nearby saying a prayer, along with her sister and a teenage boy I called the wolf man because he always tried to scare me at church. Later, when my grandparents arrived, I heard one of my grandmothers ask my mother, "Well, my lands, Miriam! Where could she be?" Soon after that, the aroma of foods brought in by the community began to reach me, beckoning me into the kitchen, but I resisted the temptation to reappear.

The moment I was discovered was the moment I'm pretty sure that baby Ken suffered irreversible psychological damage from Mama's earsplitting proclamation that she'd found me. She'd come into the nursery with Ken to change his diaper, and through the peephole where I was hiding, I sensed her urgency to return to the search efforts in the sleepy little town that was playing a huge game of hide and seek with its newest "big sister." When she opened the bottom drawer of my brother's chest, the game was over. People came running and the room flooded with relatives, friends, church members, law enforcement officers, and citizens who wanted to see for themselves that I'd been found alive.

Satisfied that I had successfully reclaimed my rightful family position, I relished that evening in the limelight, being hugged and petted by the people of Reynolds, Georgia. Once I felt important again, I decided that I would try to be nice to the new baby and let him stay. After all, I knew even at the tender age of five that I was going to need another preacher's kid in our glass house to live life alongside me. Together, we might stand a better chance of surviving the scrutinizing eyes of all our father's flocks.

CARPET FUZZ

Anyone who has ever known a preacher or is related to one knows that PKs create a great deal of stress for their parents. We are peculiar children who become bizarre adults. Often, the indicators of this inevitability become apparent early in life. Such was the case with my brother.

Shortly after Ken's birth in Reynolds, Georgia, we moved to St. Simons Island, Georgia. I guessed that Reynolds had decided it needed a preacher without any PKs causing turmoil in the town, because we moved to a new church on an island. I predicted they would welcome some excitement. Ken and I wouldn't let them down!

As we unpacked boxes, I resumed kindergarten in our new place and was constantly sick. Perhaps it was the fear of losing me again that prompted my mother to get me to the doctor right away. We learned that I needed a tonsillectomy. Our first visit to the Brunswick Hospital proved fruitful for establishing Dad's relationships within the medical community that would persist on predictably sequenced terms for the next eight years. Not long after my operation, Dad was taken oystering by some church members who assumed he knew the safety precautions necessary for the pastime. He didn't. He slipped on an oyster bed and sustained a gash so gruesome it required forty-two stitches.

Thus far, our medical troubles had been of the surgically repairable variety, and those didn't stop there. But soon, baby Ken's symptoms reared their ugly heads, forcing us to admit that our family also had to face some psychological issues as well. This occurs all too often in ministerial families, and we would not escape unscathed.

Eating the fuzz from our variegated green shag carpet that we fluffed with a metal yard rake was the first sign that something was wrong with Ken. Instead of behaving like the creeping tot that he should have been, he became a creepy, catlike creature that coughed up hairballs. We'd find him in my parents' closet, with his tongue protruding and receding behind his drooly lips, moving the fuzz around so that it tickled his tongue. Most young preachers and their wives who delight themselves by showing off their baby will lick their fingers and wipe the baby's hair into place, priding themselves on the beautiful infant-loving hearts of admiring church members. Not my parents. They were deprived of these types of opportunities and interactions because of Ken's addiction to carpet fuzz. Instead of rubbing his head and prompting smiles, their fingers were always in his mouth trying to get a hold of any fuzz that he was swirling around in there.

Because he didn't discriminate amongst carpets—any variety or color suited him just fine—we could not go anywhere that he didn't try to eat the rug. Ken rarely was held by any of the other ladies of the church, because of Mama's fear that he would cough up fuzz balls all over them, potentially prompting full-flock gossip that the preacher's wife needed to keep a cleaner house.

My parents decided to have Ken evaluated by a doctor, and the diagnosis was astoundingly simple: he was seeking from the carpet the same warmth and security that a stuffed animal generally provided other babies his age. I don't think that Dr. Lupee had ever seen such a relieved preacher! Both of my parents now had hope that Ken could break his habit if given a stuffed animal to love. On the way home, we stopped at Harper's Five and Dime in the Pier Village on Mallery Street to let Ken see some stuffed animals and gravitate toward the one he felt he could bond with. An oatmeal-colored bear about the size of a Kleenex box, with moveable arms and legs, was the winner. The bear proved to be the cure for Ken's carpet sickness.

Or so we thought. Over the next several days, we noticed that while Ken and his bear were inseparable, the bear developed a receding hairline, right smack in the middle of his forehead. The green shag carpet fuzz was merely replaced in Ken's mouth by oatmeal-colored bear fur.

Discouraged once again, my parents took Ken and the bear back for another examination by Dr. Lupee. This time, the doctor was perplexed. He paced and rubbed his chin, while my parents' feet were cemented to the examination room floor. Ken was tightly gripping his bear on the table, and my bottom was glued to the chair, awaiting the dreadful news that Ken was irreversibly damaged and could never be fixed. We were all on the verge of tears ourselves when Dr. Lupee stopped, turned around to face us, and bellowed out a heart-wrenching fake cry.

He approached the table where my brother was sitting and looked at him for what seemed like twenty minutes, and then turned his eyes to the stuffed bear, shaking his head apologetically about the bear that was prescribed to provide Ken with warmth and security. I remember thinking that Ken would probably rather be in a carpet warehouse where he could solve his own problems without the medical intervention that was being attempted.

Dr. Lupee reached out and tenderly massaged the bear's bald spot saying, "This poor bear has a boo-boo on his head! It hurts him!" He produced a Snoopy Band-Aid from his big white pocket and affixed it firmly to the bear's head. Ken was sobbing, his bottom lip quivering, obviously feeling remorseful about the pain he had inflicted on his bear.

Never again—at least to my knowledge—did Ken eat any kind of fuzz from stuffed animals or carpets after a wise doctor was able to psychologically alter his abnormal craving. Yet even now that we are adults, whenever I go for a visit with Ken, I always do a carpet check of the premises, just to be on the safe side.

THE TABLE MONSTER

If the members of a church congregation were questioned about their pastor's family, the answers would likely be unanimous that the pastor and his wife are saints who certainly could have done nothing to deserve the burden of the little devils wrought from such a kind and loving union. "The Lord never gives you more than you can handle," Miss Terwey once reassured my mother, patting her hand sympathetically.

Miss Turwey should have known because one Sunday when we picked her up for church, she and the other Miss Turwey weren't waiting on their front porch in their matching chairs like they usually did. One was washing the other one's hair in the kitchen sink because she'd mistakenly picked up the can of Raid thinking it was hairspray. She had to redo the top half of herself before church. She got through that ordeal without being overburdened by the Lord in his goodness and probably managed to kill a few unsuspecting bugs in the process. Miss Turwey and her twin sister were seventy-six-year-old spinsters who had lived together all their lives but were no longer permitted by the Georgia Department of Motor Vehicles to operate any type of machinery on the roads.

It became my dad's mission to pick the Turwey twins up for Sunday school every week. In fact, this was the reason that we upgraded our pastoral family car from an old, brown, beat-up Buick sedan to a brand new wood grain and metallic blue Buick station wagon. We needed more room. My Uncle Robert remarked that it looked more like a hearse when he saw it, and I swore I'd never ride in it if people thought it was perpetually leading the way to the cemetery. But given the choice of riding in the new car or having my tail torn up with a switch that my mother would have made me go pick myself, I chose to ride in the car, albeit with deep personal reservations. It wouldn't do for a PK to be seen kicking up a fuss in the back seat of a hearse when others would be expecting to see everything remain motionless back there, especially in the absence of heavy blue velvet curtains.

I considered Miss Turwey's words to my mother and was reminded of them daily as my loathsome brother put us through his own unique rendering of the terrible twos. In his case, they started early and ended late, not only in the overall scope of it, but in the hourly phase as well.

Ken was not a morning person. Every preacher's family has one just like that, but I escaped that curse of my own and instead inherited our dad's inability to sleep past six o'clock or stay awake past ten. Still, I suffered through my brother's nearly incurable morning plague. In the days before Carnation Breakfast Bars were invented, I liked to eat toast for breakfast. Mama would put bread slices under the broiler to toast, and I was allowed to pull up a chair and stick my feet in the oven while I waited for my toast to brown. When it finished, I'd slather it with apple butter and take it to the table. I usually got there just after

Dad, who brought his Bible and sermon notes to the table to study them over his coffee. In truth, he was more likely offering up fervent prayers that everyone would make it through the morning without a full-fledged eruption of temper. But temper always arrived anyway, carrying a little tan bear with a Snoopy Band-Aid on its head. Temper climbed up into the old, blue wooden highchair without a tray and pulled himself up to the table. There, he waited for his cereal. No one was allowed to look at him, and his objective was to watch everyone in the room closely to make sure they didn't.

Occasionally, we had houseguests who didn't know the unspoken rules that applied at our breakfast table. Aunt Peggy came in, beaming like rays of sunshine in her quilted yellow housecoat and matching butterfly slippers with the orange feathers. She made the nearly fatal mistake of looking at Ken. He growled at her like a dog with rabies and didn't stop until she took her eyes off of him.

"Felix, what's the matter with him?" she asked.

Dad looked up at her from his coffee and replied, "With whom? I don't see anyone."

Aunt Peggy was dumbfounded, but she got the point. After a few minutes of silence, she stood up and announced that she couldn't believe that my parents would let my brother get away with such rude behavior and that it must be stopped. She stomped over to our pantry and took out all the cereal boxes and brought them to the table. She lined them up around my brother's cereal bowl, making him his own wall that he could hide behind without causing any of the rest of us to have to avert our eyes from his direction. This worked well for a while, even though on particularly disturbing mornings, Ken would peer over the wall in an effort to catch someone looking at his wall. He had to check the ferocity of his growling from time to time.

Dr. Lupee cured my family's odd assortment of plagues, but the one malady that he never cured was my brother's growling. That was a job for Mama's father, DeeDaddy, who was from the old school of childrearing. He cut no slack and made no apologies. Dr. Spock would have had him committed, but Dr. Spock himself wouldn't have been able to perform the miracle cure my DeeDaddy performed on our table monster.

Over his Cheerios one morning, DeeDaddy looked in the direction of the cereal box wall and caught Ken's stare. When Ken growled at him, DeeDaddy let him growl for a minute or two, and then DeeDaddy let out the longest, loudest, meanest growl back at Ken, and held his hands up with curled fingers like a lion ready to pounce. It scared the meanness right out of my brother, who never growled at anybody again. All the prayers that hadn't worked hadn't necessarily been wasted, but it took an exorcist to get rid of my brother's breakfast demon, which never reappeared after Ken was out growled.

THE WEE ALARM

Bed wetters are a curious breed. Of course, we've all wet the bed in the process of nighttime toilet training, but at a certain age, it is no longer a toilet training matter, it's full-blown bedwetting, referred to as Enuresis by doctors and other members of the medical profession. For some kids, it doesn't take long to get their relief schedule in check. By the age of four, they have dry nights and will never wet the bed again unless they either have friends who pour warm water in their hands while they are sleeping or they dream that they are on the potty and the dream world crosses into reality. But for others, like my brother, the problem persists.

My brother Ken did nothing at the expected time. All of his baby milestones were screwed up, and he forced my mama to have to sit there and listen when all the young mothers in the church were together talking about their babies' new accomplishments. She couldn't contribute to the conversation, because Mama would never be able to one-up anybody else's child with a kid like Ken, who once had a habit of eating carpet fuzz and growling at people.

We knew something was amiss when Ken's new puppy didn't want to play with him. Ken and I had each gotten a new black poodle from a litter of puppies being offered for free to good homes. We made the cut. I named my puppy

Deacon, because it seemed a fitting Christian name for a PK's dog. Ken named his puppy Mork, after the space alien Mork from Ork on the popular sitcom *Mork and Mindy* starring Robin Williams.

Mork must have thought Ken was going to get him in trouble for peeing on the floor. Our puppies got a little newspaper paddling for mistakes when they were being housebroken, and Mork associated the smell of pee with punishment. Ken's room smelled like pee, and that's probably why Mork didn't like to go in there.

Ken liked to put Mork on the leash and walk around the house with him, but my parents and I started noticing that whenever Ken said, "Come on, Mork," and started to leave the room, Mork would slam on his brakes, causing Ken to drag the poor dog along. Ken never sensed Mork's lack of enthusiasm and kept right on going, leaving us to watch Mork, silently pleading for our help with his eyes, being dragged down the hall to Ken's room. Deacon happily stayed put, grateful that he'd been put into the right pair of hands when they'd passed out the puppies.

In her pre-retirement days, my grandmother worked for Sears and Roebuck in the catalog sales division. Pretty much everything we bought new came from Sears and Roebuck, since my mom found a way to legally claim my grandmother's employee discount. At that time, a new product hit the market. It was called a Wee Alarm, and it was designed to alert bed wetters.

I never understood how it was going to help anyone suffering from the disorder, because the alarm went off when the wire got wet. I figured it really couldn't do much good then, because it was too late once the alarm went off. I myself have tried to stop mid-stream, and I've learned that when a person really has to pee, there's no stopping it. I've also seen for myself that alarms can make people pee who weren't otherwise planning to pee, so the whole idea for the invention was fruitless, in my opinion.

But if we hadn't tried a Wee Alarm for Ken, then we couldn't honestly say we'd tried everything. So my parents bought him one for the standard twenty percent off. We tried it. It didn't work. If anything, it just made things worse, as I'd suspected it would from the get-go.

When we first hooked him up, I was afraid for Ken. At that time, I didn't realize that batteries wouldn't shock a person like electricity would, and I didn't want Ken to get zapped. But when Mom showed me how it was safe, I rested a little easier—until we were all asleep. Then, whenever the alarm went off, we all woke up and went running to Ken. Every time, we found him sound asleep. He slept right through the Wee Alarm, leaving only the non-bed-wetting members of the family alerted and wide awake.

Most PKs know that a minister needs his sleep. He has to have a rested spirit to be able to counsel people in doing the right thing and to work on his sermons. Any children in the household who go to school also need sleep to have a fresh mind for working math problems and reading well enough to make it into the next reading book with the rest of the reading group. Ken may have had all day to sleep, but the rest of us didn't.

No matter how hard I tried at school, Ken and his Wee Alarm were affecting my academic progress. The last straw was when I got a C on my report card in math. Waking up from a little catnap during math, I told the teacher I was having trouble remembering some of my numbers. She called my mama to see if there were any problems going on at home that she should be aware of in light of my slipping grades. When my teacher told her that I'd been complaining of extreme sleepiness and numerical disorientation, the Wee Alarm had given its last alert. All because my teacher had sounded her own alert—and just like the Wee Alarm, it had come after the fact.

CODE CRACKERS

Growing up in South Georgia in the home of a pastor, no matter what the religious affiliation may be, one never wants for food. But for Southern Baptist PKs, there is always an overabundance of mouth-watering delights that would make starving children in Africa think they'd died and gone to heaven. Ken and I learned from our dad at an early age to take a spoonful of each dish so that no cook would ever be offended. Southern ladies are like that, especially those with deep religious convictions. Their food is an extension of themselves, and so to reject a dish that they have prepared is to reject them personally. It's hard to understand how a the absence of a spoonful of food on a plate can cause resentment for years and even lead to bitter fights between competitive cooks, but that's just how it is in the South. This is the reason that I took a liking to every food I ever tasted and sometimes have to shop in the plus-size women's section of clothing stores today. I sacrificed my health and developed a habit of overeating, all so that no southern cook ever got her feelings hurt.

Ida Proffer reigned the queen of desserts, but Dad never told anybody except Ida herself that he felt that way, and his secret was safe with her. I had to agree with my parents. She made the best orange slice cake and English

Toffee in the South, but the sad thing is that, like most southern women, she was unwilling to share the perfected recipe with anyone. She didn't even have it written down anywhere for fear that her house help might discover it and get rich. Her recipes were in a database in her head that could only be accessed by her.

The standard by which all other desserts were measured was by Miss Ida's orange slice cake. Some of the time, other desserts failed miserably in comparison, yet the lady who'd prepared it showed nothing but unabashed pride and a fickle posture like Minnie Mouse blushing in Mickey's presence when the food gift was presented to us. I remember one such occasion when poor old Mrs. Hamner brought us a chocolate cake—bless her heart. My father eagerly accepted the covered cake plate and assured her that "cakes like this sure don't last long around here!" He was telling the truth. After she left, he took one bite and scraped the remaining cake off of the plate and into the trash. Later, when he thanked her, he quipped that he'd enjoyed every last bite of that chocolate cake. Her face radiated sheer pride. When I think back on that experience today, the teacher in me wonders what her home economics teacher would have written in the comment box on her report card. It was probably the standard encouragement, "Thelma never stops trying. Be proud of her steadfast efforts."

As every grown PK has figured out, pastors have even been known to refer to members of their flock as certain types of food. Preacher's kids become skilled Code Crackers as we mature. As I got older, I understood the secret code that my parents had developed in their conversations about people. When Dad came home from a Wednesday night business meeting at the church, he would usually inform my mama that "the turkey's been at it again."

It didn't occur to me initially that "the turkey" was the code name for snotty, tight-bun-headed Mrs. Willison, who balked at every idea and budget issue in every business meeting and tried for years to split the church all in retaliation for her messy, slanderous divorce several years before. She didn't like anything unless it was her idea, just like in her failed marriage. She had an axe to grind with God for allowing her husband to stray, and she figured the most effective place to do that was in God's own house. In one heated business meeting, she got outvoted by the members of the Amen Corner about the forthcoming inscriptions in the hymnals. She thought that gold was too haughty a color for the inscriptions, and that God would consider it tacky and not hear the prayers of any member of the church if we went through with the gold inscriptions. She was pushing for beige inscriptions.

When gold won unanimously, except for her one beige vote, she erupted with such rage that she slung the hymnal from her pew across the aisle into the Amen Corner and hit one of the deacons in the right ear, causing it to bleed. She stormed out of the meeting with her face as red as a watermelon and the veins just as obvious. The deacon with the bleeding ear stood and asked the shocked and speechless members to bow their heads in prayer and proceeded to pray:

> Father, forgive this woman, for she knows not what she's done. Let him who is without sin cast the first stone, but please don't let it be Hilda, Lord, for even though she has sinned and come short of your glory, as my wife she has proven herself on occasion to be fiercely protective, and without the restraint of the Spirit, she is likely to confront her sister in Christ, Mrs. Willison, in an ungodly way. Please be with Mrs. Willison, for whom if necessary I would respectfully honor your command by turning the other ear, just as I'm sure your good and faithful servant Mr. Willison has done many times before. And, Lord, please continue to hear our prayers, even as our hymnals are inscribed in gold, for we do this in Your honor as we strive to give only our best in Your name. Amen.

Every other member of the Amen Corner echoed.

Until I cracked the code, I just speculated that whenever Dad mentioned that the turkey had "been at it," he had gotten indigestion from some turkey he'd eaten for dinner. But I wised up when I got a little older and couldn't remember any turkey being offered as a covered dish on the Wednesday night family supper table. I started fixing my plate with an eye for turkey, and I knew that it was not offered as frequently as he referred to its effects.

It didn't take long from that point on to read between the lines and crack codes in other conversations. I was amazed at the number of parishioners who had acquired food and animal nicknames for themselves, unbeknownst to them, in their pastor's household code language. Now that I am an adult, living hours away from my parents, I take great strides to be a peace-loving church member. I sure don't want to earn myself a nickname, but I'll admit that I'd love to be a fly on the wall in the home of my current pastor. I'd love to see if the nicknames I have given some of the members are the same ones he's picked.

CHURCH CLOWN

Despite the few "turkeys" that have ruffled the feathers of the flock in Dad's churches, the overwhelming benefit of being a preacher's kid is the blessing of loving and supportive relationships along the way. As far back as I can remember, Dad has always been a highly respected member of every community in which we've lived and has been a model of inspiration for so many others. Strong, lasting friendships have been formed through the years. Most of those relationships that have stood the test of time have been with people who have a keen sense of humor.

Just as every classroom has a class clown, every church has a church clown. One such clown that I remember is Mr. Gerber. After church one Sunday, he called me over to his pew and told me he had a picture he wanted to show me. He'd folded a five-dollar bill into a perfect square, showing Lincoln's portrait. He told me to just keep that picture, because it wasn't a good picture, and he didn't like it anyway. On another occasion, when Dad complimented him on his new watch, Mr. Gerber took it off of his wrist, threw it at Dad, and told him to keep it. He explained that in some countries, like in Asia, people who receive compliments feel obligated to give the complimenter the item being admired and that now he couldn't keep the watch because he had Asian origins in his ancestry. Even though it wasn't evident in his physical features, it ran through his blood in such a way that he knew he couldn't keep the watch. My dad never complimented Mr. Gerber on anything else, and even though he felt compelled on occasion to compliment Mrs. Gerber on a new dress or hairstyle, he thought better of it because he didn't know what kind of trouble that might lead to. Dad always took special care to err on the side of caution when it pertained to his parishioners. My mother assured him that he was doing what God would expect him to do as the shepherd of the flock.

Sometimes it was hard for me to calculate just how far Mr. Gerber would go to pull a practical joke, but I always sensed that he was responsible in his choices. When I was in upper elementary school, my parents would leave me home alone on occasion with the understanding that I was not to open the door for anyone. It came as no surprise that Mr. Gerber would be the one they would ask to test me.

Just as soon as my parents had left one time, there came the knock at the front door. Strange. No one ever came to our front door. We always used the side door, under the carport.

But there he stood at our front door, wearing jeans and a plaid flannel shirt. He had on a Halloween mask missing one eye that had been caked over with skin, leaving enough of a dent that if he held his head back, the eye space might hold a quarter cup of standing water. The sight of him was grisly, but I appreciated his attempt to humor me. I opened the door a crack and shouted, "Mr. Gerber, take that silly mask off your head right now.

You're scaring me!" My words were met with his attempt to keep up the prank.

He replied, in a garbled tone that would suggest that he was an elderly drunk man who'd forgotten his dentures, "I gossa fiyawood im my twuck I wanna sell ya." Mr. Gerber's ability to make me laugh was never confined to the church. I laughed like I'd never before laughed in my life, developing a stomachache from the muscle contractions. It was just like him to take time out of his day to plan and carry out a practical joke like this one, just for me. As I continued laughing, he kept up his salesman-like pitch, never asking me what I found so funny. "See, wook im my twuck. Thessa fiyawood I got." Hooting uproariously to the point of tears by now, I was certain that when I looked out toward the road where he was telling me there was a truck with firewood for sale, my parents would be standing there shaking their fingers at me and scolding, "We told you not to open the door for anybody, and of all people you opened it for Mr. Gerber! Shame on you!"

When I looked out at the road and saw an old beat-up pickup truck loaded with firewood, my world changed forever. Part of me felt the urge to scream in fear that I could be murdered at any moment, and part of me wanted to fall on my knees and beg God and the one-eyed, toothless stranger's forgiveness for such ridicule of an elder. Ignoring both of those desires, I somehow managed to non-chalantly quip, "Come back later, gotta go." I slammed the door, twisted the center- knob lock, turned the deadbolt, put on the chain lock for added protection, and hid in my closet until my parents came home.

Being alone in the house in a pitch-black closet with a fiercely pumping heart brought me to my first real come-to-Jesus meeting. In those desperate moments of de-escalating from a panic mode, I accepted the world as a dangerous place for the first time in my life. I earned my "people-sensing antennae" from this experience of mistaken identity, and this pivotal moment continues to etch a deeper understanding of the nature of people in a church and in the world: whether a church clown, a disabled salesman, or a terrorized child, we all seek acceptance and comfort.

I never told my parents what happened with the old salesman, and I never noticed any fresh firewood stacked between the trees in our backyard that winter. Every time I see a "firewood for sale" sign, my heart melts when I think of the old man whose attempt to provide warmth was met with such fear and cold resistance. And along with those firewood sign sightings, I am reminded that it takes a lot of clowns and strangers beyond the boundaries of the church walls and pastorium to give Preacher's Kids any hope of turning out "normal."

THE CRAB LADY

Generally speaking, PKs are cheated out of an upbringing that even remotely resembles that of their non-PK counterparts. For one thing, ministers' families are often poor in the monetary sense, so we have to find cheap entertainment. The upside to this disadvantage is that preachers' kids often become highly creative, crafty people who think a lot like the special agent MacGyver, who could construct an Uzi from a ballpoint pen barrel. This cultivated resourcefulness begins early in childhood and continues throughout our lives. People who hear about clever ideas and ask themselves about the idiots who would try an insane thing like that for the first time can be assured that a Preacher's Kid made the astounding discovery.

When all my friends were at the movies, I was home playing worn-out board games that Mama had bought at yard sales, and most of which were missing a pair of dice or some other necessary game piece. All of our Monopoly pieces were replacements; I was always the piece of macaroni, and my friends could choose from an eclectic assortment that included a cufflink that had lost its mate, a Barbie radio, and a safety pin. I played with any friend who felt sorry enough for me and would agree to come over instead of joining the rest of the group at the movies. We'd borrow the dice from another board game, and we'd get along until we had an argument about one of the game rules. Mama would hear the commotion and arrive on the scene. I frequently had to be reminded that God would not have me behave in such a way with company over visiting. All PKs know that unacceptable behavior is to be reserved strictly for family time.

When my friends were skating at the roller rink, swimming at the village casino, or participating in any other event that required a fee, I was usually playing school in the backyard, writing with a stolen piece of chalk on a green piece of wood Dad had nailed to a tree for me. Sometimes I had trouble keeping on the fake fingernails that I'd made from ovals of dried glue and licked so they'd be wet enough to stick to my own short fingernails, but I kept sticking them back on, because I wanted to be just like my teacher. Being a teacher was my dream. I liked to yell at invisible students and dish it out just like I'd had to take it. The one thing I swore I'd never do was make my students hold out both arms and put a thick dictionary in each upturned hand for five minutes or until tears started to flow, whichever came last. Even for a PK who planned to someday be a teacher, this was an unspeakable act that would be too rotten to carry out on a person, even a student as foul-mouthed as Pookie Hortense. My second grade teacher didn't feel the same way about those dictionaries, though. She had no mercy and didn't want any, but her tough love managed to cure a few ills throughout the year. Mrs. Boyer and Daniel Webster saw to it that Marvin Pirtle never peed in the second grade bathroom soap dish again and that Karl Rex never felt the urge to show a second girl his one-eyed pet that lived in his pocket.

When I couldn't talk one of my friends into coming over to my house, or when their parents were making them take some time off from playing with the PK until they'd kicked the bad habit they'd picked up from me, I'd go crabbing. At an early age, I developed a healthy respect for crabs. On St. Simons, the village pier was the place to go to catch the feisty crustaceans.

Mama had five crab traps that she set up on the days that we crabbed. She'd buy some cheap chicken necks up at the village grocery, and we'd tie them into the bottom of the crab nets along with a piece of a broken brick to weight the trap down. We'd walk out about halfway down the pier and tie the traps to the railing, and then we'd sit and wait.

One thing all PKs know how to do well is wait. Most of us learned this critical life skill in the hospital waiting room while our dads were paying visits to the bedridden, but we got plenty of practice at church, too. It came in handy when I learned to crab, and I began to see the transfer of patience to different areas of my life, particularly on the pier, because crabs will not be hurried. Mama says they will sit there and watch the chicken neck for a while before they attempt to pinch part off and eat it. I guess they see too many of their friends disappear while gorging on food that seems to appear from nowhere and is too good to be true, and they want to let a buddy go first. If that buddy doesn't suddenly disappear in an upward underwater whirl, then others skitter over thinking it's safe to have a bite or two. That's when we'd nail them.

I would never tell any of my close friends this, but my mama was known as the Crab Lady on St. Simons. She could out-crab anybody around, and all the village pier regulars knew it. Would-be crabbers who were having a hard time getting a crab to turn loose of a crab trap string would send one of their children down the pier to fetch the Crab Lady to come help. Off I'd follow, right on her heels, to see the crab that was being uncooperative. Mama never failed to make a crab behave, whether it wanted to or not, and only one time did a crab get the best of her and draw blood. She knew just how to step on the top of the crab and then grab its back legs so it couldn't reach around and pinch the living daylights out of her. There were some crabs that would not be taken without an honest fight, but Mama won every time by simply pulling off the big front claws. She showed them that they weren't so tough without their weapons, and they'd realize their doom as the cooler closed on top of them when she dropped them in to spend their last few minutes with others of their kind.

When I reminisce on the days of my childhood, I have some deep regrets for my own children, who, by the way, are not PKs (their mother had the good sense to avoid any man considering the ministry as a profession). I am heartbroken that PlayStations have provided real imaginary friends for today's children, who should be out crabbing instead. I am concerned that computers have become best friends with kids who would enjoy life more and learn how to settle disagreements if they were playing a board game with a person, even if that game is missing a few pieces. Most of all, I am saddened that more kids don't play school, because they've lost respect for their teachers. But despite these regrets, I remain hopeful, all because on one of the barrier islands along the Georgia coast, a certain preacher's wife they call The Crab Lady seems to have the answers to disagreements, discipline, and so many other life issues boiled down to a science...in a crab trap.

THE KUMQUAT TREE

"Heaven help us, they've done it again!" When a preacher stumbles into the kitchen for his first cup of coffee, looks out the window at his yard, and says these all too familiar words, his family knows at once that the trees are full of toilet paper. Right away, calls are made to the minister of youth and the minister of music to see if their yards are just as Charmin-ed. There is a tiny flicker of hope that at least one of them will say yes, just so that the job of un-papering both yards may be shared. It might not seem like it would be such a chore, but unrolling a rolled yard is not an easy task. If the youth of the church didn't use quality toilet paper when they did the job, then the paper will break and remain up in the tops of trees, forcing the use of ladders to get it down before it rains and the tissue becomes an even bigger mess.

PKs have the teenagers of the church—the ones who rolled our yards in the middle of the night—to thank for our adept tree-climbing abilities. The cover design of Katherine Paterson's *Preacher's Boy* depicts Robbie Hewitt, the main character and PK, hanging barefoot from a tree. Paterson grew up a child of missionaries, so she knows her subject matter, but what's so apropos is that as a daughter of missionaries, she still chose to make the PK the main character. It wasn't only the deacons' kids accusing us PKs of being the worst—the deacons' kids were in cahoots with the missionaries' children. They ganged up on us!

Because library books are free entertainment for preachers' families who live on shoestring budgets, we are often avid readers who see parallel perspectives from the books that we read and the situations that we encounter. Books give us another way of reaching outside the strict confines of life as a PK and yet another chance to ever be considered normal human beings. I think that E. B. White, author of the beloved childhood favorite *Charlotte's Web*, had a little firsthand knowledge of PKs, too. When Fern and Avery are swinging from the high barn swing in chapter ten, White writes, "Children almost always hold on to things tighter than their parents think they will." That was true of all the PKs I ever knew, and it applied to a lot more than just our grips on trees.

I recall an oak tree that must have been as tall as a four-story building. It spread its branches in the middle of a community circle where children in my neighborhood played. There were boards nailed to the tree so that children could climb up and crawl out onto a very sturdy limb to a seat with a back made of a piece of plywood. When new kids came to join in the fun but had to try about twenty five times before they finally mustered up enough courage to go ahead and climb up the tree, I always helped initiate them. I showed them how to hold the heavy rope with the knot at the end between their upper arms and their sides as they made the life-threatening climb up to the seat. From there, they slid their bottom to the edge of the piece of plywood far out on the heavy limb and put the rope between their legs, easing the dinner-plate-sized wooden seat up toward their bottom. They held on for dear life and let themselves fall from the tree, enjoying the feeling that only a child can know on a traditional rope swing. We had tire swings, too, but we left those for the little kids, because they didn't pose enough danger to get our adrenalines rushing.

Good trees grew all around. Some had swings, some were rolled with toilet paper, and some were just good to climb and enjoy the view from above. But not all the trees of my youth bring back good memories. There was one tree of my childhood that got me into a lot of trouble, but in the end it did help me understand the problems that Adam and Eve had with that snake.

Right across the property line of the First Baptist Church, just over the six-foot wooden fence that the residents next door had erected, there stood a succulent kumquat tree. Unlike most kids my age, I happened to like kumquats. In fact, I liked them so much that I climbed the fence and picked them on a regular basis after school. The property lines of the playground of my elementary school, the church, and the yard that housed this kumquat tree all met in a Y, so when I'd climbed the fence from the schoolyard to the church, I only had to walk about fifty feet to climb the other fence and pick myself a few juicy kumquats as an after-school snack before going in to the church to get my dad to take me home.

It didn't take the resident of the house long to figure out that I was a kumquat thief. Only I didn't see it that way. Some of the branches of the kumquat tree hung over the edge of the property line, so I considered those kumquats the property of the church. Since my dad was the preacher, I had the first rights to them. The owner of the kumquat tree explained to me one afternoon when he confronted me that this wasn't how it worked. He told me—in words that would not be pleasing to the Lord—that if he ever caught me on his fence again, he'd march my little ass right into my dad's office and tell him what I'd been up to every afternoon after school. I had hoped it wouldn't come to this, but I decided to stand my ground on the encroachment issue, knowing in my heart all the while that God would surely take my side in the argument over someone who would use such bad language toward the daughter of a preacher who said such good things in front of so many people about the entire Trinity every Sunday.

I didn't see the man sneak up under me as I picked the first kumquat. His sinister voice startled me so that I had to catch myself to keep from falling off of the fence. I could have been killed! Instead of making sure that I was all right, this middle-aged man with greasy gray hair and inexcusable razor stubble reached up and pulled me down from the fence. "Young lady," he directed, "you better start sayin' your prayers right now, because when we get to your daddy's office, you're gonna need 'em."

For a man who was so despicable, I couldn't understand how he ended up being so right. When my dad realized that this was not the first time this man had issues with me, and when the man told my dad the explanation I had given him for picking the kumquats in the first place, Dad was livid. I remember Dad's calm demeanor and profuse apologies to the man, with assurances that this would not happen again—but when that office door shut and the man had gone back home, the kindness in his voice stopped like a driver at a yellow light with a cop on his bumper. Looking back, I surmise that Robert Louis Stevenson's dad must have acted like this one time, too, to have provided the inspiration for *Dr. Jekyll and Mr. Hyde*. As I reflect, I believe I saw beastly hair start to grow on my own dad's face and hands. His teeth looked more pointed to me, and his gruff voice was the dead giveaway that he was in a morphing process.

By the time we got home and the pain from my spanking had simmered down a little bit, I wished I had never seen a kumquat tree in my life. Even as an adult, when the produce section has kumquats put out, I think back to my childhood and look away from those kumquats. If I'm not quick enough about it, my rear end starts twitching.

AN UNDERSTOOD SQUIRREL

Besides being good targets for toilet paper decorations, homes for rope swings, and sources of kumquats, another feature of trees is that they draw squirrels. As a child, I received mixed messages about squirrels. I blame this on my parents and my dog. Dad and every other preacher I have ever known love all God's creatures and demonstrate this love gently and tenderly. My father's Heinz 57 dog, Ploopops, had been the almost-human kind of dog that showed him that all beasts have feelings if you look deeply enough into their souls to see.

I believe that my mother never understood animal love as a child because she grew up with Chihuahuas. She might as well have just gone on ahead and settled for cats, for that matter, because she never learned the lessons about animal love that a real dog like Ploopops might otherwise have taught her. But God always gives second chances, so he sent her Bridgett, a cross between a Schnauzer and a Poodle that we called a Schnoodle. Bridgett was almost human, too—so much, in fact, that I believe she realized what was considered a fair animal fight and what was not. She was a good Christian dog that any preacher would have been proud to own, but she was a devout Southern Baptist, so God sent her to us.

Bridgett lived to tree squirrels. She'd chase them all day, and they learned that she was usually up for a game of chase whenever they felt like playing. We always wondered what she'd do with one if she ever caught it, but when we found out, it wasn't at all what we'd expected.

Bridgett's early experiences with squirrels were seeing them skinned and cut up in a pan of water on our next door neighbor's porch. Doc Byrd loved to go squirrel hunting, and sometimes he'd cut off a little taste of his catch and give it to Bridgett. Doc Byrd taught Mama how to shoot a squirrel dead every time, but there was one occasion when I was about six years old that she must have forgotten everything he'd taught her.

I'd just gotten a brand new swing set that I promised to share with my brother. It was the Sears aluminum variety with red, white, and blue striped poles, and it had a slide. It was a fancy enough swing set for any child, but it was uncharacteristically fancy for a preacher's kid who wasn't used to having anything so new that hadn't ever been used by someone else before. Since Mama's mama worked for Sears, my parents had gotten it on clearance with a 20 percent discount on the clearance price.

The bench swing where two kids face each other and sit like they're waiting at a bus stop was the swing I was on when the unimaginable thing happened. Ken had tottered off chasing a butterfly, or something ridiculous like that, and I heard Mama holler for me to get off the swing set. She had spotted a squirrel running along the neighbor's fence, and she had the BB gun ready. The swing set was between the fence and where she stood with the gun.

Being the bull-headed child that I was and having faith that she was as good a shot as Doc Byrd, I didn't really see any reason that I should move, so I stayed put. The one thing I hadn't considered was that the squirrel was running along the fence in my direction.

That was when the BB stung my leg. My mama had shot me! As I writhed on the ground screaming in pain, I saw her running toward me. For a moment, I wondered whether she was coming out to make sure that I was dead or to make sure that I was still alive and that she hadn't put my eye out. Once I stood up, she convinced me that the BB had ricocheted and struck me at a glancing blow on the side of my leg and that it hadn't broken the skin, and I was not going to die. I wanted to call the doctor to get a second opinion, but she said she didn't think that would be a good idea, and besides, she knew her minor medical emergencies because she'd been in school to become a nurse when she met my daddy. I realize now that once she figured out I was okay, she knew that it just wouldn't do in a small Southern town to have the front page of the newspaper headlining that the Baptist preacher's wife had gone crazy and shot one of her kids when really she'd have only had to admit that maybe she wasn't as good a shot as she thought she was. But I'm sure that if things had gone that far, the deacons' children would have rallied quickly to her defense, assuring the general public that I had deserved what I'd gotten and that in fact it had been long overdue.

With such scornful feelings toward squirrels demonstrated by my mother, such animal-loving tendencies demonstrated by my father, and such questionable motives of my dog, I was really confused about where our family stood on the issue of squirrels. I thought they were cute, but I also knew that they would bite if cornered. I also knew that Ken wasn't old enough to have an opinion, and even if he did, it wouldn't have mattered—he'd have just wanted to eat the fur anyway.

I didn't have to philosophize long. My grandparents had purchased property on the Sapelo River, just north of Darien, where we went for rest and relaxation from time to time and where I sometimes stayed for long stretches of the summer. Those huge Spanish-moss draped oak trees at the river house were home to hundreds of squirrels.

Two doors down from our river place lived a family with three boys. One of the boys, Scottie, was my age. Since I was a tomboy, we got along fine. We'd take our dogs and go fishing on the dock, we'd swim in the river, we'd roll each other around inside an old tire, and sometimes, if we just felt like doing nothing or if it was raining, we'd go inside, put some salted peanuts in a bottle of Coke, and watch *Gilligan's Island*.

One morning, Bridgett came ambling up with a funny gait and dropped a hurt baby squirrel out of her mouth. Apparently, the baby had fallen out of a nest in one of the trees and had been knocked unconscious upon impact with the ground. Bridgett had known that this squirrel was not fair game for her, because it could not be chased. It wouldn't have been a fair fight for her to gobble it up or dismember it, so she did the Christian thing and brought it to us for help.

Scottie's mom knew how to take care of the squirrel because she'd worked for a veterinarian for many years before Scottie came along. She wrapped it in a clean, soft cloth and poured some hydrogen peroxide on a little open wound that she found. We were concerned about the possibility of broken bones or internal injuries. Trying to figure out whether it was a he or a she, Scottie decided that since it wasn't obvious, it was probably a she but that we'd better choose a unisex name so that we were covered either way. We decided to each make a list of names and we'd discuss them the following day. For the night, the baby squirrel stayed at Scottie's house, where his mother and nursed it with warm evaporated milk in a little tiny bottle.

By the following morning, no one doubted that the squirrel was going to live. It was unbelievably active. Scottie had put it in a metal cage that his hamsters had lived in before they died. It could climb upside down on the metal part of the top of the cage and ran around in there like it was a gymnast practicing for the Olympics.

It had to have a name, but of all the names we considered, none really seemed to fit when we said the name and then looked into the face of the squirrel. Finally, when DeeDaddy walked over to see it and asked Scottie's mother if she was going to let him keep that rascal, our squirrel finally had a name! We decided that since Rascal demonstrated more masculine tendencies, we'd regard him as a he.

Rascal was spoiled from the beginning. He was given dry corn and all sorts of dried nut and berry treats that he especially loved. He soon outgrew the metal cage and really needed more room to run around. The day came when Scottie's mother explained that it was time to let Rascal go, and that perhaps he could find his family somewhere in the trees nearby. Scottie was upset, but he agreed. We took Rascal outside and opened the cage, but Rascal didn't leave. He sat there eating his corn, staring back at us with his cheeks packed tight. We decided to walk away and let him leave when he felt ready, and not to rush him. Hiding behind a bush, we saw him hesitantly venture out and climb a tree. Our eyes were both filled with tears, and when we each saw the other crying, we looked away. Who cried over silly squirrels anyway? We decided to go to the neighbor's pond and look for snakes to take our minds off of Rascal.

Later that afternoon when we heard Scottie's mom ringing the dinner bell, we ran back to the house, where we were amazed to look in Rascal's cage and see that he'd come home for dinner, too. There he sat, eating corn again. For years, Rascal was the resident squirrel who was tame and who returned for his corn when he heard Scottie's mom ring the dinner bell. Who except Ivan Pavlov would have guessed?

The best trick Rascal knew was how to startle people. He loved to run up our pants legs and sit on our shoulders. Everyone in the neighborhood who knew Rascal expected it, but for guests who had come to visit the river house and had no clue that we had a tame squirrel who roamed the grounds, it was alarming! We were lucky that no one ever had a heart attack or hurt Rascal trying to swat him off of themselves.

One of the last times I saw Rascal, I guessed he'd been in a fight because his tail was half-gone, but he was in good spirits. Scottie showed me an area on his backside where someone had shot him with a BB gun, and the injury had left a bald spot on him where the skin was healing. I didn't tell Scottie, but at that moment, I was able to truly connect with Rascal in a way that few humans are able to connect with squirrels. For I, too, had once been shot and was still in the recovery process myself.

OFF TO SEE THE WIZARD

Books have been a part of my life since before I was born. When I was in my mother's womb, my father read aloud to me as he studied his Hebrew, Latin, and Greek texts in seminary. This may have happened with a lot of other PKs, too, because most preachers love to read. Besides their church libraries, many preachers have home libraries as well. My parents could have built our house out of books and still had some left over to fill the shelves.

Growing up in a family who loves books and all other things that involve words, I came to value all genres of literature as a young person. That was probably why I was allowed to participate in the children's summer drama production of *the Wizard of Oz* at the community theater when I was in fourth grade. Plenty of preachers would have disallowed their children to be in such a play, arguing that there is no moral or spiritual value in such writing, but my parents valued imagination and freedom of speech. They not only supported but also encouraged my desire to be in the play. This was one more opportunity for a PK to be out of the parsonage, a fledgling at large among the normals.

Auditions required solo singing. I had to sing "Somewhere over the Rainbow" in front of a panel of adults casting the play. Most every girl who tried out wanted the role of Dorothy, but I didn't. I knew my limitations, and singing was one of many. All those hymns I ever sang in church didn't help polish my voice or enable me to carry a tune, despite my wholehearted efforts. Judging by the looks on their faces, I sensed that the judges picked up on my weakness and that I wouldn't get a role. But I kept my hopes up and said a few prayers, and I got a phone call. I would be a green girl in the Emerald City. I was ecstatic! That was a step up from a Munchkin.

Rehearsals took all summer. I ate, slept, dreamed, and breathed the play over and over in my mind. I dreamed it so much that my dreams of the play seemed like reality, and reality sometimes seemed more like the dream world. It was sometimes hard to tell the difference.

Most of the cast was children, but the two witches, Dorothy, Scarecrow, Tin Man, and Cowardly Lion were teenagers, and the wizard was an adult. Two girls were cast as Dorothy. The director said that this was a good idea because they agreed to take turns, and if one Dorothy got sick, the other Dorothy could fill in. Both girls had beautiful singing voices, so I could understand how it was hard to pick just one Dorothy in the first place. There was no live Toto. They just stuck a black terrier stuffed animal inside a wicker basket.

Preparations for the play were soon underway. The cast dyed big Fruit of the Loom T-shirts green for the emerald girl costumes. We wore green tights underneath. Green headscarves completed the look, and one of the moms sewed sequins onto them so they sparkled under the stage lights. My favorite part of the whole costume was the glittery green eye shadow that went clear up to our eyebrows. The Munchkins' costumes were big T-shirts, too, but theirs were all different colors and had flowers on them. The Munchkins did not get to wear glittery eye shadow, but they did have cute little hats with flowers protruding from their rims.

Industrious mothers worked together to design and sew costumes for the main characters. I learned about working with others and how reliable we all had to be to commit to a role that required practice and a lot of hard work, even before the audiences began to appear.

On opening night, I was so excited that my parents were there to see me perform! I was going to make them proud. The community theater had given them free tickets to get in, as they did for all clergy. It was the Christian thing to do. It was also a gesture of reciprocity, since the theater might someday need clergy members to defend a certain production on scriptural grounds. I've seen that happen.

That first night wasn't our best performance, because we were all jittery. Our performance was good, except that two of the Munchkins got into a dispute over where their assigned spots were in their circle on the stage, and one Munchkin ended up pushing the other one down. When the fallen Munchkin got up, he chased his aggressor off of the stage during the singing of "Follow the Yellow Brick Road." They were caught by a stagehand, taken backstage, and reprimanded. Both of those Munchkins were suspended from participating in the play the following night. From then on, they knew exactly where they were supposed to stand.

A couple of the performances in the middle of the run were plagued with a mishap or two, as well. Tin Man's legs were made of cylinder-shaped pieces of thin metal that had been welded together for the thigh and the shin, but those two pieces were joined together in the middle with a coffee can so that Tin Man could bend his knees. The coffee can was slightly bigger than the shin piece but smaller than the thigh piece. Somehow, the three pieces on one of the legs nested in such a way that they became unbendable, causing Tin Man to trip and fall during his rendition of "If I Only Had a Heart." When he tried to get back up, he couldn't get a foot underneath himself, so Scarecrow dragged him offstage for a vertical realignment.

Another time, when Cowardly Lion was supposed to jump back away from Dorothy when she told him he ought to be ashamed of himself for scaring Toto, he missed his mark and jumped clean off the stage, landing in the lap of an audience member seated on the front row. Dorothy carried on as if nothing had happened while he apologized to the startled patron and made his way back up onstage.

Dorothy probably knew to carry on that way because she knew how Cowardly Lion felt when he made his mistake. She herself had tripped over her own feet when she did her side skipping down the yellow brick road a few nights before. She was almost behind the curtain when it happened, so a lot of the audience probably missed it. Ironically, the only cast member on his way to see the Wizard who never made a mistake during the entire run was Scarecrow—and he thought he was the one who needed a brain!

None of these mishaps was as serious as the one that happened on the final night of our performance. The Wizard wasn't there for the cast roll call before the show began. Every cast member was worried that we'd be Wizardless, but the director assured us that he was probably stuck in traffic or something and that she was sure he'd be there in time for his part. He did arrive on time, but when Dorothy, the Tin Man, the Scarecrow, and the Cowardly Lion arrived at the Emerald City and went in to talk to the Wizard, they were in for a surprise. The Wizard of Oz was drunk, and we had no alternate Wizard.

It didn't take the audience long to figure out what was going on when the Wizard began. His words were garbled and his speech was slurred as he boomed, "I am the great and powerful Lizard, and who are you?"

He was supposed to give Dorothy and her three pals time to respond and tell why they had come, but the drunken Wizard added a line. He said, "Never mind, don't tell me, I already know who you are."

Cowardly Lion, Tin Man, Dorothy, and Scarecrow all turned, confused, to look at each other and then at the director, who was behind the curtain on the other side of the stage. They were looking for answers to the predicament, but the answers didn't come quickly enough.

Tin Man was supposed to explain his need for a heart, and the Wizard was supposed to respond by calling him a mangled pile of junk. Instead, the drunken Wizard, in his obnoxious state, didn't wait for Tin Man to say his lines. He blurted out, "What do you want, you oily piece of shit?"

Everyone in the audience gasped, and the director ran out onto the stage, yelling, "Cut, cut!" When the lights came on, the director apologized on behalf of the community theater for the Wizard's behavior and added that any young children in the audience should not have been subjected to language like that. As she was making her impromptu speech, a very involved parent who had stayed for most of the rehearsals and who knew the Wizard's lines made her way back behind the shower curtain where the Wizard had been stationed before he suddenly realized the magnitude of his mistake and fled the scene. She likely made history as the first female Wizard of Oz when she finished the play in the drunk Wizard's absence.

Remarkably, the show had gone on, and we had a final night that we'd never forget. It even made the paper the next day, along with a photograph of the whole cast lined up across the stage, holding hands and taking a bow. The originally-cast Wizard did not appear in that photo, but the accidental one did. The original Wizard was probably back in the merry old Land of Oz, where he'd been when the play started, having another drink and celebrating the end of his run as the Great Wizard.

As a Preacher's Kid seeking to be a normal kid in a cast of apparently purposeful misfits, I wondered, is there really a normal? Am I there yet? Will I ever be, and most importantly, *do I want to be?*

CHICKEN POX

Whenever I'm getting to know someone and I tell them that I grew up as a PK, they usually ask me what it was like growing up in a preacher's house. Since it was the only experience I ever had, I can't fairly compare it to someone else's experience that I never knew. But I do tell them what Saturday nights were like. That was my favorite night of the week.

Saturday night was soaking night. I took baths during the week, but on Saturdays I soaked. Mama made sure I stayed in the tub for a good thirty minutes on Saturday nights, and usually she coaxed me into being agreeable about it by letting me get into her bathtub—which was bigger than the one in my bathroom—and by adding some bubble bath. She said I required a good soaking because it wouldn't do to have the preacher's daughter in a new dress with dirty knees, and that my knees needed extra time to get clean.

Saturday night was the only night of the week that I washed my hair, because it was down to my waist and took a long time to dry. Once I got out of the tub, I'd wrap up in a towel and Mama would put me under the hair dryer. We had the beauty shop kind with the cushioned seat and the helmet-looking top that lifts up and down like a toilet lid and has air holes. Mama's beautician, Miss Winnie

Mae Finch, gave it to her when she closed her shop and moved into the nursing home. Mama said it had strings attached, but I never found any.

I hated having to sit there for so long, but it gave Mama time to put the finishing touches on our Sunday dresses before I had to stand there turning around slowly and letting her pin the hemline. While Mama hemmed our dresses, we always watched the *Lawrence Welk Show*. I loved to dance around the room when the bubbles fell from the Lawrence Welk studio ceiling, and I developed an affinity for polka music that far exceeds the chicken dance. Dad could never be in the room while the *Lawrence Welk Show* was on, because he had to be able to hear himself think.

Mama made us mother-daughter dresses from matching material a couple of times a month. She is a very talented seamstress, and she tried her best to teach me how to sew, but when we got halfway through a pair of terry cloth shorts that were my first project, she saw that she had her work cut out for her. Like so many other PKs I've known, I wasn't an easy child to teach. I required every ounce of her patience, and the only things I ever perfected were wrap-around skirts that didn't require any buttons or other notions.

There was a girl my age named Hillary Sprite whose mother also made mother-daughter dresses. Hillary's mama was a deacon's wife with an active bladder, so her family always sat on the front pew because it offered easy access to the restroom through the adjacent side door. Mrs. Sprite could move virtually undetected from her pew during the service any time nature called.

I'm not sure if Mama and Mrs. Sprite ever had any kind of sewing competition going on between the two of them, but I do know this: one Sunday, when Hillary's mama knew that my mama and I were going to be wearing dresses that would rival theirs and probably win for a change, she called our house to say that Hillary had come down with the chicken pox and that my brother and I should be brought over at once to spend some time with her.

There was an agreement between our families that the first one of the children to show spots would be expected to intentionally infect the rest of us. It was said to be the curse of the devil himself to suffer from chicken pox as an adult, so before the invention of the chicken pox vaccine, the obligation of God-fearing mothers was to make sure that their children became diseased to go ahead and get it out of the way when a mild case could be more comfortably endured.

The Sunday of our beautiful dresses would have to wait. We got to miss Sunday school and church for four weeks in a row! The first week, my brother and I were taken to the Sprites' to contract the disease, and the following week I was beginning to show spots. As expected, my brother wasn't as quick to show spots as I was, so we eked out a couple of extra weeks at home between the two of us before we were both all dried out, scabbed over, and ready to venture back out into public places again.

I don't remember what happened the day that Mama and I wore our prized keepsake dresses, but I do remember that a few years later, when I had become skilled enough to make myself new reversible wrap-around skirts to wear to church every other Sunday, Hillary was in sewing school making her own polished cotton dresses with English smocking and zippers. She still sat with her family on the front pew every Sunday in church, so that she was easily seen in all of her spiffy handmade frocks. The ladies of the church ranted and raved about Hillary's handiwork, and everyone was proud of her clothing creations. But I also know that there were an awful lot of prayers being said for her, in the hopes that the one chicken pox scar that was right between her eyes wouldn't last too long.

SECTION C

When God created Eve, he knew that he'd have to make her tougher than Adam would ever be. And to temper her toughness, he threw in some extra scoops of tenderness so she could keep him under control one way or the other. When she was complete, God saw that this was good. But I believe that he went back and improved his recipe for the women that he would fashion as preachers' wives. These women are a premium blend of ingredients specially-designed to help temper preachers' rage in private. They are the ones who go before others to bring their husbands under control before they let them out of the house.

PKs have shocking stories about the miracles that their mothers have performed in their homes. Any preacher alone would have trouble keeping his wits about him in a distressing situation. Especially if that preacher is a diehard sports fan and discovers that someone has been messing with his Sunday morning *Atlanta Journal and Constitution* before it ever even makes it into the house—or worse yet, stealing it.

For as far back as I can remember, sports statistics and the crossword puzzle are the two staples of the morning newspaper for the preacher I call Dad. True to the adage that one never realizes how important something is until it's gone, Dad's missing newspaper proved the intensity of his feelings for it.

Since I was still in the awkward stage of awareness of what went on around me, and so much of it still went right over my head, I wasn't aware that there was a problem until the pattern emerged. When I heard an ungodly word or two (okay, more than two) coming from the kitchen, and Dad was making no attempt to hide his anger and clean up his choice of words, I was like a paperclip being pulled toward a powerful magnet. Unable to resist the urge and always one with the need to know everybody's woe, I hurried to the front of the house to get a better eavesdropping perspective on my parents' conversation.

"The **bleep** sports section had been missing every **bleep** Sunday morning for three blasted weeks. And the **bleep** sections that weren't important anyway but that were left there had dog pee and dog**bleep** all over them." I didn't have to use my code cracking skills to figure out what was happening.

Dad made a stakeout plan to solve the mystery. The following Sunday, outfitted with a heavy quilt spread out and a cup of coffee to keep himself from dozing off, he set up our camp on top of the washing machine and dryer, which were under a window that allowed an unhindered view of the end of our driveway. The paper was due to land there just a short time later, barely within the boundary of illumination provided by the corner streetlight. Dad's mission was to part the curtains just a tad and keep his eyes on the paper so that he could watch it the minute it hit the ground. We theorized that the paper boy wasn't going to sling it out there in an already-violated state. I felt like Nancy Drew.

Dad's speculation was that there must be someone working on the early shift at one of the factories in nearby Brunswick who simply couldn't afford a newspaper. Surely this shift worker had randomly chosen the green house with the black shutters as one that looked like it wouldn't have a sports fan to miss section C, and he considered our newspaper his for the taking. Dad further predicted that the paper was then peed on by a dog out on its morning trot a short while later. Most dogs are house trained on newspaper, so naturally the roving dog would gravitate toward the target at the end of our driveway and take aim.

For a preacher who is trained to detect sin in all its forms and who had already helped some notorious sinners seek forgiveness and make restitution for their actions, Dad had—and still has—a lot of trouble accepting the reality that some people are just downright evil. He refused to admit that there could be anyone heinous enough to steal a person's sports section and then stand there whistling in the calm of the early morning while his dog defiled what was left.

A few cars drove by before daybreak, but there were no takers. No one even slowed down. A jogger ran past, unaware that his every step was being scrutinized. A little old man walking a white toy poodle came creeping along, but the twosome didn't raise any dander.

"It would have to be somebody able to get away pretty quick, and a dog that could put out more than that little bitty thing," Dad confirmed.

We'd almost given up, and my discouraged Dad was headed back to the coffee pot for a refill. My protests had convinced him to wait it out a little while longer. As he poured his coffee, I turned to watch the fluffy puffball bounce on down the street. Where had they gone? They were just at the corner a minute ago.

I heard the pop of a rubber band and looked back in the direction of the newspaper, but it wasn't there! By that time, Dad had heard my gasps and wasn't going to waste time peering through gaps in the curtains to find out what I was seeing. He threw open the curtains and spied the culprit that had finally taken the bait and had it spread out on the ground reading it.

The poor little old man and his poodle were both oblivious to their having been caught in their crime, even as Dad was halfway down the driveway. I stayed inside with the door open in close proximity to the telephone, just in case someone was going to have to call the police. I figured I could give them the scoop and describe the suspect that they would need to apprehend, if it came to that.

When the little old man looked up and realized that Dad was right there, he attempted to make chit-chat about the Braves winning a game and asked Dad what he thought about Nock-A-Homa and Toot-Toot Peanut Butter—the beloved mascots of the Atlanta Braves at that time. But Dad was too smart for that. He already knew that the Braves hadn't won. Furthermore, he wasn't going to divulge his feelings about Nock-A-Homa and Toot-Toot Peanut Butter at sunrise on the Lord's day to a total stranger he'd just caught stealing Section C. Dad calmly said, "I am very disappointed in you for what you've done," the way a modern-day parent might say to a child who has colored on the wall with a box of Crayola's different brilliant colors.

Like most dogs that have a sixth sense in similar situations would have done, the poodle took a step back when the little old man rose to his feet and shook his finger in my dad's face and said, "Now listen here, you just better be careful who you're accusin'!"

Dad held himself together much better than I thought he would. "I'm not accusing. I'm telling you that I know you're the one who's been stealing my paper and letting your dog pee on the part you leave here. This is no coincidence, sir, and if my paper goes missing again, I will file a report with the authorities." And with that, Dad picked up his paper and came inside.

I admit that I was disappointed. I wanted to see that little old man get slugged by my dad, and I wanted to run out and kick his dog. But that was not to be, thanks to the prior interventions of my mother. Dad got his coffee and took his paper to the kitchen table and sat down and started reading.

Later, we found out from a neighbor (who always said you could never trust a Yankee) that the little old man with the poodle was a gambler from New York who frequented the dog races. He wasn't a Braves fan and probably didn't care about any baseball team at all. He was only concerned with which bets he'd won or lost, and he figured that Nock-A-Homa and Toot-Toot Peanut Butter might help him disguise his addictions.

Thieving old men and swearing preachers may not have ruled the day in the lives of my non-PK friends, but I was beginning to accept the reality that the normal I enjoyed was far more exciting than the normal my friends knew. Who else got to play Nancy Drew in real life alongside a detective preacher father? If this spelled normal, I was satisfied!

LOST HER MARBLES

My parents have collected antiques since they were married, and they have an insatiable appetite for a bargain. Preachers generally do. That's why my parents travel across the South to choose pieces of furniture with histories. They love to tell visitors where things came from and who owned them.

Mama's aunt Madelle spilled her coffee early one Sunday morning when she learned about the chair she occupied. She and Uncle Raymond had come for the weekend to see Dad's new church and to see how big my brother and I had gotten since the last time they saw us. We were sitting in the living room where the good furniture was, instead of in the den. In the South, when company is visiting and they're talking, it is only proper to sit in the living room—away from the television—to show respect.

Aunt Madelle wasn't even the one who asked the question that led to the dreadful coffee burn on her left leg. Uncle Raymond was responsible for that. When there was a brief lull—which happens with relatives who have lost touch for a little while—Uncle Raymond made the mistake of asking, "Miriam, where did you get that chair?" He was referring to the one with the lion paw feet that had marbles as toes and held Aunt Madelle in her housecoat, sipping her coffee with the aromatic steam swirling out of the cup.

"Oh, Felix and I got that in Valdosta. You wouldn't believe the story behind that piece! It actually belonged to Dr. Wallace Peacock and his wife." Directing her words to Aunt Madelle, she explained, "He was the psychiatrist who treated our cousin Willorene."

Aunt Madelle asked a clarification question for Uncle Raymond's benefit to help him remember the names above Willorene's on the family tree. "Oh, you mean Willoretta and Dean's daughter? The crazy one?" Willorene had been named by blending the first part of her mama's name and the last part of her daddy's name.

"That's right," Mom continued. "When Dr. and Mrs. Peacock's children had picked over all they wanted and settled their grievances with each other about who got what, this chair ended up on the auction block as part of their estate. It sat for years in Dr. Peacock's waiting room. His children didn't have any bones to pick over their dad's office furniture, so they let all that go. I ended up with the winning bid for this piece. Felix and I re-covered it, because the upholstery was dry-rotting from sitting in storage."

"So, it's likely that Willorene spent a lot of time in that chair, eh?" asked Uncle Raymond.

"Oh, I'm sure she probably did," assured my mother. "Whether or not it was this exact chair she was sitting in the day she was discovered sitting naked as a jaybird waiting on Dr. Peacock to finish up with the patient ahead of her, I don't know, but this chair was in the room when that whole scene took place. I like to think it was Willorene's host chair that day."

Everyone in the family knew that Cousin Willorene went through phases where she wouldn't take her medicine for a little while, just to check and see if she was well yet. Dr. Peacock had gently explained to her in her state of undress that she'd have to go back on her meds, because this wasn't something that would be considered acceptable by people who walk around in full wellness and that if in fact it had been any other office that she was sitting in at the moment, she'd have been arrested for indecent exposure and taken to jail. Willorene didn't argue with him. She walked over to the coat stand and agreeably put her coat back on, then sat back down and continued waiting for her scheduled appointment. Unfortunately, it was one of the last appointments that she would keep. The next time she went off her medicine, she just gave up.

"The flowers on Willorene's casket were some of the prettiest I'd ever seen," Aunt Madelle said. "I always did like magnolias in the mix; they freshen things up a bit."

The craftsman in Uncle Raymond threw out the burning question, "So did you have to do anything else to it, or did you just reupholster it?"

"Yes, God rest her soul, we did do one other thing" my mama said. "When Felix and I were trying to figure out a way to hide a flaw on one of the lion's paws, we decided to carve out some little sockets and put the clear marbles in as toes. Lots of chairs have that, so we thought it would be a good solution. We did it in Willoretta's honor, because she always described Willorene's condition as having lost her marbles. Felix and I decided we'd fix up that chair so that if her spirit ever paid us a visit, she might just find her marbles after all. And do you know that once I sat here admiring that chair, and every one of those marbles lit up?"

And that was when Aunt Madelle flipped her coffee cup.

Uncle Raymond and Aunt Madelle didn't stay for church. Aunt Madelle's thigh was burned so badly that she said she couldn't wear her pantyhose, and good Christian women didn't just show up in God's house without hose, because it was considered sacrilegious where she came from. She and Uncle Raymond asked if we could mail them some pictures of the new church, and they headed on back home to tend to Aunt Madelle's burned leg in a less formal setting. A few years later, we heard on the news that the lady who is responsible for all of the restaurant chain coffee cups having to remind us in written legal terms, "Caution: Contents Hot" had suffered a severe coffee burn and become an instant McDonald's millionaire. We considered Madelle's burn scar our missed opportunity for failing to interpret Willorene's enlightened idea.

STRANGE BIRDS

In the handful of churches that my dad has pastored in my lifetime, I've come to know some eccentric people. PKs the world over know these same types; only the names and faces change. The unforgettable ones—the good, the bad, and the downright weird—all had secret code names that were known only in my household. There is one lady who still stands heads above all others as a strange bird. She sealed her fated code name "the Dodo Bird" somewhere along Interstate 95 when she was helping transport an oak buffet that my parents had purchased at an antique shop in Sylvania, Georgia.

Mrs. Poppell stood over six feet tall and had blonde hair and legs as skinny as a blue heron's. She needed some dental work that she'd never gotten, but judging from all appearances, she probably never even realized that she needed it in the first place. She and her husband lived in a yellow single-wide mobile home in Druid Oaks Trailer Park on the other side of Brunswick. Mr. Poppell was one of those men who swore he'd never set foot in a church and kept to his word. He never wore anything except those ribbed sleeveless T-shirts that showed off his collection of tattoos but failed to keep his chest hair under control.

Mrs. Poppell liked to come to our church because Dad had counseled her after an abortion that she'd undergone a few years before. She had found forgiveness and was assured by my father that his flock embraced all believers who had sinned and come short of the glory of God. Including her. Our church was one of the few bright spots in Mrs. Poppell's life, so she arrived every time the doors opened, driving a great big red Ford pick-up truck that was nice and shiny on the outside despite a few dents but reeked with the foul odor of cigarette smoke on the inside.

On Sundays after church, people file out of the front doors and tell the pastor either that they loved his sermon or what they thought was wrong with it. One morning when Mrs. Poppell was speaking with Dad, his eyes lit up when she told him that she would be absent from church for the next two Sundays. She and Mr. Poppell were going to visit his family in Athens that week and hers in Sylvania the following week. Mr. Poppell was between jobs and they had time on their hands.

Dad asked her to wait until all of the people were gone so that he could talk to her about a moneymaking opportunity for herself and Mr. Poppell. She gladly waited, and after a while had agreed to pick up a heavy piece of furniture that my parents had bought in Sylvania. They were having trouble finding a way to get it home it, but it had been too good a bargain to pass up. Mrs. Poppell said that she and Mr. Poppell would be happy to bring it home with them when they returned and that they would do it for free, but since Mr. Poppell was between jobs, the fifty dollars would sure come in handy.

Dad gave her directions to the store where the oak buffet was and told her that he would call the owner of the store and arrange to have a few men available at the scheduled pickup time, because the piece was so heavy that it would take more than just Mr. Poppell and the owner to get it in the back of the truck. So it was all set, and my parents were looking forward to getting their new buffet.

Every Redneck "if" Jeff Foxworthy ever mentioned was true of Mr. Poppell. In fact, Mr. Poppell himself may have been Mr. Foxworthy's divine inspiration. There was nothing that Mrs. Poppell did right, in her husband's opinion, so she just didn't do much. Then again, neither did he. Their lack of ambition and upward mobility explained their complacency with the monthly welfare check. Mr. Poppell never missed an opportunity to let Mrs. Poppell know that he was the man and he wore the pants. Whenever they went anywhere on a trip, he always drove because he thought women drivers were stupid. Mrs. Poppell wasn't used to doing any interstate driving at all, and she proved it on the way home with the oak buffet.

Mr. and Mrs. Poppell had planned to pull out early the next morning and head home from her parents' house, so they'd picked up the buffet the evening before, and had covered it with a tarp in the back of the pickup truck in case of rain. But something happened later that night that caused Mrs. Poppell's parents to throw Mr. Poppell out of the house when he was drunk. They refused to let him back in. He couldn't drive and finally quit fighting Mrs. Poppell on the issue once he passed out. She had the keys, and her daddy helped her move her no-good, lousy, unemployed husband into the passenger seat. With nowhere else to go, she decided to drive home.

She remembered the way to the interstate and figured she'd just follow the signs home. She knew she had to be careful because of the buffet in the back of the truck, so she took it slow and easy. But a little while later, she got confused as she approached a truck weigh station, because she didn't know if the oak buffet exceeded the maximum weight that was listed on the sign. She said it was clear at that point, when she saw the sign that said All Trucks Next Exit, that she was supposed to exit, because she was driving a truck. She'd have to get weighed before she could proceed down the interstate.

It had been a busy night for trucks on the interstate, and Mrs. Poppell said she really got tired of waiting in that long line, but that she was making good money to see that the buffet got safely delivered. All it would take would be one ticket for failing to be weighed to make the whole venture profitless, so she just put down the windows and sat there waiting. She kept moving up toward the front of the line as other trucks made their way through the checkpoint.

Mrs. Poppell figured it was as good a time as any to clip her toenails. She turned on the light in the cab so she could see what she was doing, and propped her foot up on the steering wheel. The light woke Mr. Poppell up, and she said he just sat there looking at her for a little while, trying to focus his eyes or something like that.

All at once, when he finally realized where they were sitting, he clenched his teeth together and cut his eyes at her. "Get the hell out of here!" he shouted at her. Sandwiched in between a line of eighteen-wheelers in a red Ford Pickup with a piece of furniture loaded in the back, Mrs. Poppell eased on out of the line and went around all the semis to get back on the interstate and continue on her journey home. She says that Mr. Poppell still wonders what those truckers were saying on their CB radios as they sat there and watched the dumb blonde in the bright red truck clipping her nails and waiting her turn to be weighed.

She and Mr. Poppell came the next day to deliver the heavy oak buffet. After she told Dad the story about the weigh station and she and Mr. Poppell had gone, my parents came unglued. They must have laughed without saying a word for a solid hour, and even after that, they would read each other's mind and burst out hooting all over again. My dad said that if she'd had a CB, her handle would have been "the Dodo Bird," and this is how bird-legged Mrs. Poppell acquired her secret code name from her preacher.

CLOGS

Life isn't always happy in the homes of PKs. We endure some trials that children in most other households wouldn't begin to understand. We see the harsh side of life at an early age, no matter how hard we may try to close our eyes and ignore the life that goes on around us. Total strangers call our dads in the middle of the night, while others just decide to wait out the night and bring their problems to our doorsteps the next day. In many ways, our awareness makes us better people as we learn from the mistakes of others. But there is still the embarrassment of learning from the mistakes that we inevitably make as we grow up.

Wooden clogs are weapons and as such should be banned from schools. Crystal Shanks, fittingly dubbed the Clogged Kicker, tormented all the students in my class and made it hard for us to focus on our studies without having to worry about where she was and what she was thinking.

Most every day after school, I walked to my dad's office, which was just on the other side of a fence at the back of the school playground. When I got there, he took me home. Because the school was fairly close to my house and I could have walked home if I'd had to, there was no bus route in the neighborhood where the parsonage was located. This is why I walked home one afternoon when Dad was tied up with someone who was having a crisis in his office.

Crystal Shanks walked to and from school every day because her grandmother didn't have a car. I didn't realize just how poor they were at the time, but I found out later that she wore those clogs to school every day because they were the only pair of shoes she owned. Crystal and her grandmother lived on the other side of my neighborhood. When she saw me walking along behind her that afternoon, she slowed down and waited on me. I could tell that she was upset. She'd been teary-eyed all day, but she didn't have any friends who cared. Now I was about to have to find out what was eating at her.

Milledgeville, Georgia wasn't far away, but it might as well have been on the other side of the world. Some people probably wished that it had been. In Milledgeville, Crystal's mother was serving a life sentence for fatally shooting her daddy and his girlfriend. Until yesterday, Crystal had thought that her mother would be released on parole, but the parole board didn't think that was a good idea.

According to Crystal, it had all happened when she'd lived in Savannah. She and her mother had come home from a visit at her grandmother's house a day earlier than her father had expected. When they pulled into the driveway and Crystal's mother saw the yellow Firebird that wasn't theirs, her mother hadn't even turned the car off before tearing into the house. By the time Crystal's feet hit the front steps, the first shot had already been fired. A bloody blonde lay naked in the middle of the floor. Not a few seconds later, her father had fallen victim, too. Fearing for her own life, Crystal ran into the woods and hid until the police showed up and took her mother away in handcuffs. The only family left to raise Crystal was her grandmother. When I finally made it home, a lot of things about Crystal's behavior made more sense to me. I understood, and I sympathized. Now I was ready to be her friend.

My parents knew things about Crystal's situation that I still didn't know. I told them what Crystal had shared with me, and Dad oddly remarked that he was proud that I was growing up. However, he refused to allow me to go over to her house. Crystal would have to come to ours if we wanted to play. There was no explanation other than that this was the way it had to be.

The day Crystal kicked me in the shin with her wooden clog we'd been having an argument about Elvis. The one thing that her mother had left Crystal was her entire collection of Elvis albums and memorabilia. Maybe that was why Crystal got so angry when I said I didn't like Elvis. Perhaps she thought I was making digs on her mother when I said I thought Elvis was a pervert and my parents did, too. Whatever the reason, she just hauled off and kicked me as hard as she could.

When I told Mama what had happened, she just hugged me and said, "Be glad that you have parents who love you. Life is not as easy for some of your friends as it is for you." Mama might as well have told me that tomatoes were on sale for five cents a dozen down at the village pier. I didn't really think she was considering how I was feeling, but I sure sensed that she felt sorry for Crystal. That made me mad! No one was going to kick me with a wooden clog and get off Scott-free.

We had a little pow-wow when Dad came home. After Mama told Dad why I was upset, the three of us sat down in the living room. "You know why she kicks, don't you?" Dad asked me. I couldn't believe it. He didn't think I knew that she kicked people to get her way and show power.

"Crystal kicks because it's what she knows. Her grandmother doesn't discipline Crystal the way your mom and I discipline you and your brother. You and Ken may get a spanking from time to time, but we spank in love only when it's necessary, and we don't leave marks. Crystal's grandmother punishes her when she is mad, and your mom and I know that she abuses Crystal by kicking her. Have you ever wondered why she never wears shorts when all of the other children are wearing them? It's not just because they can't afford to buy her any," Dad sermonized, hoping to give me some added perspective. Child abuse. What a revelation!

Even though I was beginning to understand a lot more about Crystal, and I felt kind of sorry for her, I still knew I was going to get back at her for kicking me. If I didn't, she'd do it again and again. It had to be stopped, and I could see that it was going to take a PK to do it. No other child would have been as heartless.

Armed with my new knowledge that Crystal's grandmother would kick her when angered, I figured that the best way to make Crystal pay for the huge bruise on my shin was to make her grandmother mad. The quickest way to make her mad was to steal Crystal's lunch tickets. At thirty-five cents apiece, a strip of five of them for the week cost a dollar and seventy five cents. I would have to strike on a Monday.

All weekend, I worked up the courage to go through with it. I'm sorry to say that in the end, I did. First, I planned to bring my own lunch to school all week. Then, on Monday morning, when I went to sharpen my pencil, I took a folded piece of paper with me. I made a little detour and reached into the front pocket of Crystal's book satchel and took those five lunch tickets. I put them inside of the folded paper and tucked it inside my pocket. A few minutes later, I told the teacher I was about to wet my breeches as I marched in place. Given permission to go, I hurried down to the girls' restroom at the end of the hall and ripped the folded paper and lunch tickets to shreds. Then, I lifted the plastic wastebasket liner and dropped the evidence underneath.

I knew I'd be the first one to get searched. As I had predicted, Crystal pointed the finger at me. I tried not to seem too eager about emptying my own book satchel and turning my pockets inside-out. I even offered to take off my shoes and show inside my socks! The teacher knew I didn't take those lunch tickets. Besides, I had brought my own lunch to school.

While the rest of the class ran around the room looking for Crystal's lunch tickets as if hunting for a golden Easter egg, I cut my eyes in Crystal's direction and kept them there. Ha! I'd evened the score, and we both knew it. After school, on the way out the door, I couldn't resist whispering hatefully, "I have lots of friends, and they sure do a good job of looking out for me!"

It wasn't long after I got home from school that the phone rang. My mama called me into the kitchen. I already knew who it was, but she thought she had to tell me. She said that Crystal's grandmother was on the phone and that she was upset about the stolen lunch tickets. She claimed that Crystal told her that I knew who took them and wouldn't tell.

I stood right there in front of God and my family and lied. I told Mama it wasn't true. I added that if Crystal's grandmother wanted to know who did it, then she should probably talk to the teacher, who had searched everybody. If anybody knew who took those tickets, it would be Mrs. Klaus. And then I went back to my room. After she hung up, Mama came in and told me that Crystal's grandmother hadn't believed me and that I'd better be telling the truth.

The guilt started to nibble at my conscience. Not only had I made a bad choice, I felt like I had made my own mama a sinner unaware. Later that night, I set out to make things right, at least for Mama's sake. I dug out a buck seventy-five from my piggy bank and my new red, white, and blue Keds sneakers with the bells on the shoelaces, and I put them into my satchel.

The next day at school, I sat near Crystal so that I could keep an eye on her. At reading time, Mrs. Klaus told us to get out our books and turn to the first page of our new story. When Crystal opened her reading book, a piece of paper fell out. I let Griffin think he was the first one to see it. "Hey, look, everybody!" he announced to the class, "Crystal found her lunch tickets!" Mrs. Klaus just sighed and shook her head, a knowing sign that some things would never change.

Getting a new pair of shoes isn't a frequent occurrence for a PK, especially ones whose parents cut every possible corner of the family budget. But I'd managed to talk my mama into buying me a pair of the hottest kids' shoes on the market, on the grounds that I wouldn't misbehave for months, and that everybody else had a pair, including Hillary Sprite, the deacon's daughter. That was all it took.

Something made me not want to wear those shoes the first day I had gotten them. I had already been plotting to misbehave. So when the bell rang that afternoon, I met Crystal out by the tire swing.

I dug the unboxed but brand new tennis shoes out of my bag and offered them to her. "My Mama said that she thought these shoes would look nice on you," I told her. "All the girls want a pair, and they'll want to know where you got yours. Just tell them a friend bought them for you. And by the way, I'm glad you found your lunch tickets."

Mama wasn't mad that I gave the shoes away when I told her that I wanted Crystal to have them. Crystal and I were friends from then on. I helped her make some other friends by including her in our games and schemes. She never kicked me again, but she did go after some of the other kids from time to time. The rubber soles cushioned the blows in a way that the wooden clogs never had. I only wish I had found an occasion to give her grandmother a soft pair of slippers.

TOUGHSKINS

PKs whose moms or dads were also raised as PKs are known as double-PKs. My dad is a PK, but he isn't a double-PK like me, because his grandfather had more sense. When it's all taken into account, the bottom line is that my brother and I have some potentially schizophrenic genes. It's a wonder that either of us is still walking around loose in the world, especially with some of my dad's shenanigans. If it's true that the future generations pay for the sins of the father, then Ken and I are in for a rude awakening any time now.

Dad wasn't a kid who was rotten to the core like I was. He was merely behaviorally challenged, and that was mostly his cousin Porky's fault. They were joined at the hip, sort of like Barney Fife and Andy Griffith, only both of them were more like Barney than Andy.

In the railroad town of Waycross, Georgia, in the 1940s, when the roads weren't paved and air conditioning didn't happen, boys wore cutoffs and went everywhere barefooted in the summertime. The schoolhouse still had one room when Dad and Porky were in grade school, so they had the same teacher for several years. If they wreaked havoc in the classroom even once, their reputations as troublemakers would be like shadows, which sometimes precede and sometimes follow, but always stick.

During the school year, the boys had to save their cut-offs for wearing after school and on weekends. On school-days, they had to wear shoes and a shirt—and jeans. Sears Toughskins were the way to go, because they survived as hand-me-downs no matter how many kids were in the family. Other than fire, there wasn't much that could destroy a pair of Toughskins. The fabric was so thick that even a rattlesnake couldn't have penetrated it! But Porky was an exception to most rules, including Toughskins.

One morning, Dad and Jerry, another boy in the class, set out to play a joke on Porky. When they arrived in their class and Miss Lott was still writing their work on the chalkboard, they were able to sneak to the back of the classroom and steal some paste from the supply closet. Once in their seats, they secretly covered the seat of Porky's desk with a thick coat of paste before he arrived. When his Toughskin-clad bottom hit the seat, there was no sensory awareness that anything out of the ordinary was happening, until it was too late.

All morning, Porky worked diligently on his school-work, and before long it was time to go home for lunch. Miss Lott required students to turn in their schoolwork before leaving. As Dad and Jerry had known, this was Porky's day to take up the papers. But when the teacher called on him to complete his task, Porky couldn't move. He was stuck to the desk.

The teacher gasped in horror when she figured out why. "Who did this?" she demanded to know, her fists clenched by her sides.

Jerry raised his hand. "I think Felix did it. I saw some paste in his desk." He had ratted Dad out and pinned every bit of the blame on him. Dad really should have known that Jerry was a troublemaker when he had gotten in trouble for his one-sentence response to an essay question the previous year. When the teacher asked the students to write an essay explaining what they would do if they won a million dollars, Jerry's response was matter-of-fact: "If I won a million dollars, I'd buy myself a new butt, because mine's cracked."

Miss Lott marched back to Dad's desk and produced the empty container of paste. She dismissed everyone else for lunch except for Dad and Porky, who didn't have a choice in the matter.

"Felix Haynes, what got into you? How could you do such a thing? I'm sending for your mother!" But Miss Lott didn't have to send anyone. My Meema Haynes arrived at the school in a matter of minutes the way news traveled in Waycross. She was boiling. Steam was coming out of her ears, and fire flamed from her mouth when she spoke.

"Miss Lott, I'm very sorry for what Felix has done," she began. "I would like for you to impose the stiffest punishment that you can think of on my son, and his daddy and I will support it fully. But I'd like to request permission to take him home and teach him something about how the board of education applies to the seat of responsibility before you get started." Miss Lott knew precisely what my grandmother was about to do, but Dad was confused.

He didn't stay confused long. The seat of responsibility, he learned, was his own rear-end, and the board of education was the wooden paddle with holes in it that educated children in such a way that they would remember the lesson for a long time. There were no Toughskins thick enough to protect my dad's bottom from the wrath of my grandmother. He'd be sore for a month of Sundays.

The worst part of the punishment was yet to come. When Dad got back to school, Miss Lott met him at the door and took him to the principal's office. The pair of Toughskins Dad was wearing was given to Porky. For the rest of the week, Dad had to wear Porky's Toughskins. They were hanging on a wall peg, a huge hole in the bottom that Miss Lott had made when she'd cut Porky out of his desk.

CHURCH PICNIC

Important people in PKs' lives include parents, siblings, grandparents, and other extended family, parishioners, and teachers. Schoolmates, however, are generally the people to whom we related most closely when we were young. Those school friends whose families belonged to our church were likely at the top of the list of the most influential people in our day-to-day lives.

I remember wanting to be just as cool as Teddy Perkins. He was a few years older that I was, and he was the most popular kid in the church. He was good looking and well mannered around adults. His most memorable feat was the day he climbed the greased pole and won the twenty-dollar prize.

Our church was having a dinner on the grounds after church. Instead of eating indoors, the ladies of the church had set up picnic tables and spread heirloom quilts on the grass for families to eat outdoors. Queen Elizabeth herself would have been underdressed for this gala; all the women wore hats, pearls, and long white gloves with their Sunday best. I wore the daughter dress in the pair of mother-daughter dresses that Mama had made for us. They were white with orange and pink flowers in the print. Mama had bought me a new hat, a pair of gloves, pink ribbons for my braids, and a pair of black patent-leather Mary

Janes with a pair of ruffle socks to achieve the full effect. All the other little girls had on white patent-leather shoes, but Mama said that the black ones were the proper color to be worn, even in the summer, because patent-leather by definition is a summer shoe material, and the white ones looked gaudy to her.

On the day of the picnic, when we were all dressed to the nines and just as well-behaved, I was appalled to see a dead pig laying spread-eagle on the food table with an apple sticking out of its mouth. It struck me as being a rather unclean table decoration for such an upscale event. Then I saw someone stab it with a fork and take a chunk, and I knew it offered more than the average centerpiece. It reminded Karen Youngblood of Wilbur, the beloved pig in *Charlotte's Web*, and made her cry.

On any normal Sunday, she'd have been given a Kleenex and told to get over it, but the men all had handkerchiefs in their pockets that day, and each wanted to have a reason to offer his hankie to someone in distress. Karen escalated from a whimper to a cry to an all-out bawl and had to be carried away from the table where the roasted pig lay. One of the ladies fixed Karen's plate and brought it to her, but she said she couldn't eat anything and started the whole act right from the beginning again. I'd have guessed she'd have worked up a pretty good appetite after all of her howling, but she didn't touch her plate.

I think the hoopla over the pig was what reminded Teddy and his friends of the time that they'd had a greased pig chase. Our church youth group and others from around the state had attended a Youth Retreat in

Statesboro the previous summer, and the memories of the pig chase were still fresh in their minds. A boy from a church in Screven had caught the squealing pig after so many others before him had absorbed most of the grease onto their own clothes and bodies. The pig was then hosed down and returned to the pen where the farmer kept it, scarred for life after being chased by so many teenagers whose intentions were unclear.

Before long, Teddy and his friends had left in a few cars and returned to our picnic a short time later wearing cutoff shorts. Some of the girls even had on their God-forsaken halter tops, right there in the churchyard! They carried a large can of Crisco over to the flag pole and gathered around it. One of the boys climbed to the top of the pole, deposited a twenty dollar bill that he weighted with a rock, and then proceeded to grease the pole on his way back down. I found out later that Mr. Gerber, our resident "church clown," had donated the prize, because he was the one who had given them the idea. The winner was the one who could make it to the top and retrieve the money.

One by one, the group of teenagers ran toward the pole and leaped up onto it, but all who had tried promptly slid right back down. Dodd Wheeler, a scrawny redhead with a buzz cut and black-rimmed Coke bottle glasses, thought he'd better go ahead and give it a whirl before Teddy decided to try. He took off his glasses and backed up like a gymnast about to vault and tried to look just as professional. For onlookers, it was a lot like watching a doomed plane take off. Dodd hit the pole head-on with such force that it broke his right jaw and knocked out an incisor and a bicuspid. For a couple of weeks afterward, he walked around with his mouth wired shut and drank banana milkshakes with added protein through a straw.

When Teddy stepped up to the pole, the picnicking congregation turned their eyes in his direction and stopped their conversations, knowing that he was the one most likely to make it to the top. We were all surprised when Teddy didn't take a running leap. Then, we saw his strategy. He took off his shirt and wrapped it tightly around the pole. As he made his way up, he pushed the shirt ahead of him, cupping his hands so hard that it wiped the grease off as he went. When he finally got to the top, the crowd went wild. He was the superhero!

But he was also my hero for another reason. Teddy didn't keep that twenty-dollar bill after all. He did the Christian thing and gave it to Dodd Wheeler, to help his parents with the dentist's fee. The world needs more people like Teddy Perkins to inspire us all to give until it hurts.

MEEMA'S LETTERS

When Dad told his mother that he felt "the calling" into the ministry, she cried and left the supper table. Dad's father was proud of him, though. He was happy that one of his boys was following in his footsteps; his other son, my Uncle Greg, would never be taken seriously in a pulpit. He'd already spent too much time running in the other direction.

After Dad married Mama and graduated from seminary, Meema Haynes settled down and accepted what she couldn't change. Dad had become a husband and a preacher, in that order. Accepting another of his roles wasn't as difficult for her. Shortly thereafter, he became a dad. For a woman who'd headed down the dirt road to her mother-in-law's house when her own first baby needed changing, Meema had changed her outlook on infants by the time I was born.

As I was going through some old scrapbooks and memory albums, I found some of the cards and letters from Dad's parents that my mother saved for me. One with a cute puppy on the front was written to me before my first birthday (shortly before I could read), when Dad was preaching at a church in Louisville, Kentucky, as he completed seminary there. Here is what it said:

Wed noon
Cold in South Georgia

Dear Kim,

I'm thinking about you today because it's cold here and there's six inches of snow in Chicago, and you're not too far from there and there's probably some snow where you are. There's some as far down as Atlanta. Since you are a little South Georgia cracker you might not like that cold and snow, if it gets too cold for you come on down South and we'll take care of you. You could ride "for free" on the train or even a plane. Your grandparents sure would like to see you, even your Uncle Greg.

Love,
Grandmother H

My grandparents lived through the Great Depression. They knew how to be frugal. My Meema made all of their clothes, except for Sears Toughskins for the boys and suits for my grandfather. I remember once when I was visiting, I kept hearing the water turn on and off. This went on long enough to pique my curiosity. When I asked Granddaddy what was happening, he explained, "Georgia Lee's taking a shower." In order to conserve water, Meema would get wet, lather up, and then rinse before moving on to another section of her body. No wonder she got so cold when it snowed.

Meema and Granddaddy Haynes weren't the type of grandparents who gave presents in big boxes with bows. They celebrated occasions like birthdays and Christmas in more financially progressive ways. My first birthday card—the one with a little girl and a turtle on the front—explains it best:

> July 6, 1967
>
> Dear Kim,
> The little girl on this card can't get this turtle! I bet you could! Grandma Haynes didn't make you a pretty dress for your 1st Birthday, but your mother makes you such pretty ones I was afraid you wouldn't like one I'd made! When you get big enough to fuss about clothes, the length, etc., Grandma will make you one then. So we'll put some money in your account at the Credit Union. Maybe you can use it sometime when you get older and have a big date (Have your hair fixed for a date). A special one like your aunt Ann is doing this weekend. We sure can't wait to see you. I hear you've been stepping around slowly. Speed up and we'll go for a stroll one day soon. We love you very much.

(This card wasn't signed with their names, but had a Credit Union receipt for five dollars tucked inside).

As I got older, I could read the cards and letters by myself. Like most other kids, I enjoyed getting something in the mailbox, even if it took me a little while to read it on my own. Meema's letters always made me feel good. She knew how to make sad or sick people feel so much better. When I broke my right arm—I broke both of them at different times, but the right arm was by far the worst—she gave me a reason to look on the bright side:

> Kim,
>
> We're really sorry about your arm. We'll have to find something you can do with your left hand. I hope it doesn't give you a lot of pain. We've been thinking about you.
>
> Love, Grandmother and Granddaddy H.

I wonder how many other preachers besides my dad have presided at their own mother's funerals. In April 2003, my Meema Haynes died after suffering from Alzheimer's disease for many years. Her death was bittersweet for our family; we were relieved that her suffering was over, but sad to say good-bye with such finality.

At the funeral, Dad recalled touching memories as he laid his mother to rest. She'd interviewed for a job in a cigar factory once Dad, Aunt Ann, and Uncle Greg were all in school. When the manager asked her why she wanted the job, she pointed to the college diploma hanging on the wall and replied, "So that my children can get one of those." I knew how important education had been to her. She and Granddaddy Haynes had paid my way through college so I could have one, too.

PKs know that they can always count on their fathers to shatter an otherwise stable demeanor. I was proud of myself for doing so well at her funeral—my emotions in check and under control. I knew that as long as I didn't try to say anything, I could just bite the inside of my bottom lip to keep from crying. Then, on the way out from under the tent at the graveside, Dad stopped me by putting his hand on my shoulder. He looked straight into my eyes and said, "She was a good mother. There's a lot of her in you." It was as if a crystal vase had fallen onto a tile floor.

Occasionally, I stop and consider Dad's words to me. I would like to believe that I can raise my own three children as successfully as she raised hers. I hope that I can lift the spirits of those whose are down. I would love to keep the sense of humor that I think I got from her. If my son ever tells me that he has felt a calling into the ministry, I too will cry. But the words I'll remember the most came from Meema in a letter.

I am a South Georgia cracker.

A COMFORTABLE RIDE

Church youth groups channel PKs' energy into meaningful experiences. Anyone who has ever been a part of one remembers a myriad of events—some inspirational, some embarrassing, some funny, some scary. When our church youth group went to Florida one time, our whole youth group learned about patience and tolerance.

In the 1970s, a radio station in Jacksonville, Florida, had a disc jockey known as the Grease Man. He was a favorite in the region. We could pick up his station without any static on St. Simons. I never saw the Grease Man, but I would have recognized him if I had—forty years old, greasy salt and pepper hair, four hundred pounds, six-feet-tall, fat lips that were always wet like the sound of his words, wearing a torn, dirty T-shirt and cutoff jeans, with bare feet and dirt under his toenails and fingernails, disgusting ear potatoes. Listeners didn't need a photograph. His voice drew the picture.

Tuned in to the Grease Man all the way down I-95, our church youth group was piled into three station wagons making the trip to go tubing down Ichetucknee Springs. Dad was driving ours. Terry Bufkin, Brenda Clements, Lisa Lee and I were all in the back seat. Dad and Jim, the youth minister, were in the front. They had Sherry Sims sitting between them, because she didn't know any of us.

Her aunt and uncle made her go on the trip while she was staying with them for the summer. It didn't take us long to figure out why they made her go.

At first, we were all impressed with Sherry's apparent maturity. Her long, blonde, wavy hair was pulled back with a barrette. She wore a tube top and a pair of hot pants with her flip flops. The mothers in our church didn't let their daughters wear tube tops. Sherry didn't know any better for being a hussy.

Dad and Jim would pull Sherry out of her shell and help her warm up to the rest of the group. Trying to figure her out, my friends and I sat back and listened as she told them about herself. She lived in Atlanta and was going into sixth grade. She had lots of boyfriends but had forgotten all their names. And her mother let her wear a face full of makeup. Where we lived, girls didn't wear makeup until high school, and even then it was only lip gloss and face powder.

When there was a lull in the conversation, we were silent. We wanted Sherry to keep talking so we could keep listening, because she seemed to know more than we did. But the Grease Man's slimy voice turned her attention to the radio. When a song came on, she sang. She knew every word.

"Wow," my dad said when the song was over. "You know all the words. And you have such a beautiful voice." Dad was good at making people feel important.

Sherry thanked him and sang the next song with increased volume and expression. Everyone listened. She didn't miss a word.

As she kept singing, my friends and I started talking. We were excited about tubing down the river. Insane people come from all around to rent black inner tubes and jump into the icy cold water to float for two hours on tubes, three, four, and Five-man rafts, and canoes. We were planning which type of float we'd get when Miss Priss turned around and glared at us from the front seat for interrupting her solo.

Dad and Jim sat staring straight ahead, oblivious to the scornful look. Someone had created a monster. I could tell Sherry's singing was getting on Dad's nerves, but he would have never said so.

A couple of times, Jim and Dad asked us questions, thinking that Sherry might stop singing. She didn't. Changing the radio station didn't help, either. She knew country songs, too. In his rearview mirror, Dad could see us rolling our eyes.

Relief was coming. At the next exit, Dad pulled off at a gas station. Terry, Brenda, Lisa and I got out and went in to use the restroom. When we got back to the car, Dad was speaking with Mr. Robinson, another station wagon driver on the trip.

"I got to thinking that it might be more comfortable if Sherry rode in your car," he explained. "Having to sit up front between Jim and me can't be much fun."

Mr. Robinson agreed, and Sherry grabbed her bag and climbed into his car. It wasn't easy, but my friends and I contained our excitement until we got back on the interstate.

"You really think she'll be more comfortable in the car with all those boys?" Jim asked my dad.

"I don't know about her," Dad replied, "but we sure will."

FRIENDSHIP

As a PK, I wasn't allowed to see many PG-rated movies. The first one I ever saw was *The Towering Inferno* at Lanier Plaza in Brunswick, Georgia. I didn't know who O. J. Simpson was, nobody had any idea who he would become, and even if they had nobody would have believed it. Dad was a football fan, so he enjoyed O. J.'s screen appearance. The character in the movie I still think about is the fat lady who swam through the tunnel. I wonder if I look like that underwater when I swim—that is, when I'm not too scared to go into the water.

Which movie changed an entire generation of lives the most? A poll of people based on the years of their births would yield different answers. One group would no doubt vote for *Gone with the Wind*. Another would surely vote for *The Blob*. My generation will tell you that *Jaws* ended life as we had once known it.

On June 20, 1975, the classic feature film *Jaws* was released. Our church youth group went to see it together. Sharon Neddles sat next to me, and we shared a large bucket of buttered popcorn until the woman's bones washed up on the beach and the crab was crawling on what was left of her hand. If we'd know that we were going to lose our appetites so early in the movie, we could have saved our popcorn money for something else. Neither of us has been the same ever since.

As I saw it, *Jaws* did us a favor. It forced vacationers to head for the mountains instead of the beaches. The summer of '75 wasn't crowded on St. Simons Island, Georgia. Swimsuits ran seventy-five percent off, and beach balls and rafts were returned to the factories. No one wanted to tempt fate.

I used to think that things wouldn't have been so bad if we hadn't lived on an island. As I talked to so many of my friends and classmates, though, I began to realize that Jaws had an impact on people no matter where they lived. Fear wasn't limited to the ocean. Lots of us were afraid in the swimming pool. A few of us stopped taking baths and started taking showers, keeping one eye focused above just to make sure a great white shark was not being birthed through the shower head.

The commercials dared, "Just when you thought it was safe to go back in the water…" and then there was the theme of death. They didn't say, "Just when you thought it was safe to go back in the ocean or to the beach…" The advertisers were far more clever. They didn't limit the fear zone to one type of water.

Sharon Neddles confided to me once that when she tried to go back into the ocean, she got as far as the surf and started hearing the music. She was sure that it wasn't just in her head. It scared her so much that she couldn't wash dishes in the kitchen sink for fear that the shark would come up through the pipes and bite off her hands.

Whenever a life-changing experience occurs, the people who share those moments develop a special bond. That's what happened to Sharon and me. We got to be very close friends because of a mechanical shark that scared the piss out of us.

Only one fight between us ever took place after we saw *Jaws*. Our teacher should have known better than to let us sit next to each other anyway. All we ever did was talk. I don't remember the cause of our classroom fight, but we were having an argument that made me reach over and pinch a freckle off of Sharon's arm, prompting her to grab a handful of my hair and yank it out.

When our teacher got to us, Sharon had a handful of my hair and a bleeding arm. Even though we were both in pain, neither one of us wanted our parents to find out about our fight, because we'd get in worse trouble at home than we would ever see at school. Sharon lied and I went along with it. She told the teacher that her fingernails had gotten caught in my hair, and when she tried to get them loose, she accidentally stabbed herself with the point of her pencil. I don't know how her explanation worked—particularly since her fingernails were bitten to the nubs—but it did. By some miracle, we did not get sent to the principal's office.

When I broke my arm, Sharon kept me up to date on what happened in our class and on our softball team during my recovery. I saved a card with a brown cow on the front that she sent to me. It said, "How Now?" Inside, she wrote:

Dear Kim,

When I heard that you got a broken arm, I didn't believe it. But when everybody started talking about it, I believed it. You must be going through a lot of trouble. I mean when they set it wrong. And had to operate on it. You must have been in pain. Well enough of that mess I have to finish my purse. The rings are bigger then the purse. Jeff J. got knock in the head by Kassler by his skateboard. He got eight stitches. You should have seen the boys on 50's day today. They had put water in there head to make it look like greese and a box rolled up in there sleave. We won our first Pirate's game today. Tuesday we got beat by one point. I might be down to see you because my grandmother is in the hospital. When my mom is with granny I'll come see you. I am so sorry you won't be here the rest of the year. Well, I have to go now. Love you lots.

Sharon

P.S. I might have a baby sitting job.

Babysitting jobs, movies with the church youth group, new hairstyles (angel wings), macramé purses with handles bigger than their rows of knots, school, softball games, and some pinches, pulls, breaks, and scars cemented my friendships of the 1970s. No matter where we were born, PK or not, the movies that change our lives will vary, but the common thread through all the changes we experience is friendship.

As a preacher's kid in the south, the feeling that I was unlike all the rest of my friends permeated every fiber of my being. The older I got, the more I recognized aspects of my life that were vastly different from those of my friends. I wasn't sure whether this was a blessing or a curse, or a mixture of both at different times. One thing for which I am eternally grateful is the impact that others had on my life. Where would I be had it not been for teachers and parents I feared, movie-going friends and a softball team I cherished, and classmates who truly understood how to prevent worse consequences?

THE MAGIC OF KETCHUP

Pastors spend a lot of time in hospitals. Sometimes, they are seeing about members of their flock who have fallen ill, given birth, or gotten injured. Occasionally, pastors visit vacationing patients, too, if the hospital paperwork indicates a religious preference. Dad visited the Baptist vacationers. And then there are some times that preachers visit their own family members.

Accident-prone PKs make hospital visitations convenient for their dads. While Mama waited in the emergency room with me on more than one occasion, Dad scooted up to another floor and said a prayer or two and saved himself a return trip to the hospital.

When I was a baby, I rolled off the couch and broke my collar bone. I don't remember it, but Mama said I screamed bloody murder and that she felt like the worst mother in the world. When I was four, I was running with a glass of chocolate milk and fell. I had to have twelve stitches in my hand. In kindergarten, I had to have a tonsillectomy. By the time I was in grade school, Mama knew that I was a high risk, so she took out the twenty-four-hour school accident insurance with the dental clause on me each year.

Third grade was a rough year. Dad got a lot of impromptu visitation done that year, plus a nice Christmas insurance bonus for all his extra efforts. He and Mama ended up a few dollars ahead from the extra school policy coverage. For starters, I slammed my finger in a car door when coming home from the pool. The middle finger on my right hand was broken, but all I got was a splint because they don't cast fingers. I was so disappointed; a cast would have brought me more sympathy. Since I couldn't hold a pencil to write, though, I didn't have to do any of my school work except reading for a few weeks.

Soon after that, my first broken arm—the left one—happened over near the big community oak tree where we risked our lives swinging on a rope swing from dangerous heights. My friend Penny lived adjacent to the circle, so we thought it would be fun one afternoon to climb up on her roof and shout across to the kids swinging from the tree. We pulled a ladder to the front yard, and I volunteered to go up first.

Penny had a hyperactive younger brother named Peter who had no sense whatsoever. As he ran around front to see what we were up to, he collided with the ladder and brought me down on top of him. Penny's older brother, the one with some sense, put my broken arm on a pillow and walked me home.

I didn't want to get Peter in trouble, and I wanted to be able to play at Penny's house again even though there were usually no adults home when my parents thought that there were, so I lied about how the accident happened. I told my parents that I was running and fell. The doctor knew it could not have happened the way I said it had.

When the truth came out, Mama said I made her and Dad look like child abusers by lying like that. When Peter's mother found out what had happened, she tore his tail up. Not only did I have my arm in a cast, I was preached at and put on restriction from playing with all friends for two weeks and at Penny's house for forever.

Ken and I usually knew the reasons that church members were in the hospital. Sometimes, as with the birth of a baby, the news was happy. Sometimes it was tragic, and at other times it was downright funny. On one of my third grade emergency room trips to the hospital, Dad confessed to us that he'd had to back out of a parishioner's hospital room in the middle of a conversation to avoid laughing in her face.

It happened when he was visiting a widowed church member whose back was thrown out. She was an elderly lady who sang in the choir. Her secret code name was "The Cow," because of the way she tilted her head back and flared her nostrils when she sang. But that isn't the main reason she was given that code name. If a churchgoer really wants to get on a pastor's nerves, smacking gum in the choir will do it. "The Cow" proudly sat in the choir every Sunday, directly behind dad's left ear, chewing her cud. When he got to her hospital room that day, Dad asked what had happened to her.

"Well," she explained, "I went to go to the bathroom, and I saw that my shoe was untied. While I was down there close enough to it, I bent over to tie it and I sneezed." The story took a while for Dad to tell, because he kept going into laughing fits every time he tried to tell us what had happened.

The worst broken bone I have ever had happened in fifth grade. I'd been on horses regularly at Sea Island Stables. So many kids on St. Simons—myself included—had their birthday parties there because the stables had a private party room, and then after cake and presents they had people who put the kids on horses and led them around the ring.

Down at my grandparents' river house, I met a girl who had a horse in the yard behind her trailer. When she asked me if I had ever ridden, I told her that I had a lot of experience at riding horses. She brought out the horse for us to ride, but there was no saddle. We were going to have to ride bareback. Ever the forerunner, I insisted on going first.

The main problem was that the horse didn't know me. When I hopped up there, I didn't have any time to grab hold of the mane before the horse bucked me off. My forearm snapped like a dry twig into a right angle. As my friend took off chasing the horse, I straightened my broken limb and walked home cradling it. I didn't lie about how it had happened this time, but the doctor and insurance company called the owners of the horse and the neighbors anyway, to compare notes. After a drunk driver hit me a few years later, the school accident people refused to renew my school insurance coverage. They told Mama they'd never seen one kid get hurt as much as I did.

Through all of the broken bones, operations, and stitches, my most harrowing experience didn't require a trip to the emergency room. There was already a doctor at the function. It happened during my rough third-grade year. My family was at a wedding reception cookout at the Coast Guard Pool after Dad had performed the ceremony.

In the South, we call all soft drinks "Cokes." Sprite is Coke, Pepsi is Coke, and even root beer is Coke. The only drink in a can that isn't Coke is beer. I'm not sure what kind of Coke I was drinking, but we didn't have pop-tops back then. We had pull-tabs that left a pear-shaped opening in the top of the can.

Toni Meeks was the one who put her finger in the hole of her Coke can and then pulled it back out. She said she didn't think I could do that. She was right. Mine got stuck.

It didn't hurt putting my finger down into the hole, but twisting it to get it back out was going to cut. After I'd tried to figure out another way to get it out of there but could not, I panicked when I realized my predicament. Adults nearby saw what was happening and got Mama to come over. She was used to this kind of thing. When she tried to help, I put my can behind my back and wouldn't let her touch it.

Dr. Lumpkin was a guest at the wedding reception. Even though he was a ladies doctor, he said that he helped out little girls from time to time. In fact, he said he was a professional at getting children's parts out of tight places. There was a magic trick that only doctors knew. Ketchup.

Down South, we put ketchup on everything—hamburgers, steak, chicken, eggs, bread. Why couldn't it be used for emergencies? I held out my can, and Dr. Lumpkin examined it while someone went to grab a Heinz bottle from the table.

After squirting a ring of ketchup all around the top of my finger, Dr. Lumpkin began gently working my finger out of the hole. It hurt a little, but I believed in the magic once I saw the progress. My finger was coming out!

Having successfully extracted my finger, Dr. Lumpkin was applauded by the crowd. When he cleaned up my finger with a wet cloth, I could see that it was cut in a couple of places. It hadn't hurt that much until I saw the blood. He put some medicine and Band-Aids on my finger and told Mama that she didn't owe him anything. Having witnessed the doctor's trick firsthand, everyone at the reception saw that the magic of ketchup is its unique ability to conceal blood. There are those of us, though, who still believe that it has divine extricating powers.

HOLIDAY INTERRUPTIONS

Interrupted. That's how holidays can be described for PKs. Our lives are riddled with interruptions, but we're not allowed to use that word when we talk about the holidays. We're not permitted to say that Easter was interrupted by Mr. Paul's funeral or that Miss Jill's wedding interrupted our Valentine's Day. Our parents remind us that we should be grateful that we are not the ones saying good-bye to a relative—or worse, getting a new one by marriage.

Sometimes, the only way a preacher can enjoy a relaxing holiday is by leaving town and insisting that an associate minister or chairman of the deacons man the fort. The preacher misses out on a lot of free food deliveries, but nothing will go to waste just because we're not home to eat it. If the ladies of the church know ahead of time that the preacher is planning to spend a holiday elsewhere, then many of them will do their baking early. They'll deliver the goods already packaged and ready to go.

I liked getting travel foods much better anyway, because it helped cut back on the fruit baskets. The ladies didn't give fruit for road trips; they made things that would freeze so that if we got too much, we could stick some of it in the freezer and eat it when we came home.

Anticipating that possibility, they wrote their names in permanent marker directly onto the aluminum foil or container, because gift tags would fall off in the freezer. They made sure we knew where things came from!

Going out of town was a certainty for my family on Thanksgiving for two reasons. First, Thanksgiving never snuck up on a Sunday. Dad always preached a Thanksgiving service the Sunday before the Thursday holiday so that people didn't have to hurry back home before their turkey had settled. Second, Rich's in Atlanta opened at 6:00 a.m. for early bird specials the day after Thanksgiving. Mama and Aunt Ann had to stake out their spot in line.

All my aunts and uncles have lived in Atlanta all my life. We rotated hosts each Thanksgiving so that nobody felt put out year after year. The host cooked the turkey and dressing, but the other family members and friends brought the rest of the food. Mama always volunteered the dessert so that she wouldn't have to cook. She'd unwrap a cake that a master cook had given us and put it on a fine China cake dish as if she'd made it herself. So many Southern women keep recipes top secret that Mama never had to tip her hand when someone asked for the recipe. If a non-family member requested it, she'd lean over and whisper, "I'm sworn to secrecy. The governor's wife gave this recipe to her minister's wife, my good friend Betty. I had to promise Betty that I'd never give it out." Mama knew how to impress.

High noon marked the blessing time. We liked to start early so we could eat all day. One year, our interruption was a guest who just didn't get it. My uncle Greg brought a Yankee with him. Meema Haynes tried to talk him out of it, but he wouldn't listen. He never did. He said that Alice would be welcome or he would not come. That poor woman got chewed up and spit out by my Aunt Ann not ten minutes after being introduced to the family.

"Why do you people eat Thanksgiving dinner so early?" Alice asked. It was if someone had uttered the name E. F. Hutton. We could have heard a pin drop.

"I beg your pardon?" my aunt replied with poisonously sweet Southern charm.

All over Greg's face was written, *I wish I'd listened to my mother.* He knew there was no chance of recovery for Alice. She was doomed. *Kaput.* Over.

"I'm just not used to eating Thanksgiving dinner until later," she answered, oblivious that she had committed what is considered a major social faux pas in the South.

My Aunt Ann spoke through pressed but smiling lips, a demeanor discernible only to true Southerners. "Well, then, I suppose you must be used to eating Thanksgiving *supper*. In this home, we eat Thanksgiving *dinner*. Of course, if you prefer to wait to eat later, there'll be plenty left over for you."

Alice and Uncle Greg managed to delay the blessing no longer than it took Aunt Ann to deflate Greg's date. Right after the plates were cleared from the table, Greg took Alice and left. No one has let him forget that day.

Gnashing her teeth at guests before the blessing on Thanksgiving Day wasn't something that Aunt Ann did regularly. Usually she and Mama saved that for the following day. On the biggest shopping day of the year, the two of them would get up long before dawn and fix a Thermos of coffee while the car heated up. Dressed in running shoes and warm up suits, they honed in on Lenox Square, pumping the coffee into their veins all the way.

Either Dad or Uncle Tom would drive the power shoppers there so that they could be put out at the front door to get in line. They couldn't be bothered with finding a parking place. When they needed someone to come get a load of purchases and take it back home, they'd call from a payphone and one of the men would meet them at a door with the car.

Ministers' wives are generally nice people, except the day after Thanksgiving when there are sales deadlines. They will knock you down. No peace on Earth, no good will toward men.

Sometimes Mama and Aunt Ann would meet my cousins and me at the door to the mall if the men wanted to do a little shopping on their own. This usually happened in the afternoon, after the men had gotten plenty of gift hints throughout the day. One year, they took us to Santa's Secret Shop in Rich's. Shopping has never been easier—or more affordable.

Santa's Secret Shop had elves that took children to shop for their family members so that their parents didn't have to fake being surprised by the gifts on Christmas morning. Each child was assigned a personal elf, who took the little customer into the secret shop with a checklist of family members that the child was supposed to buy gifts for. There was also a budget line. Mama filled out my list and gave it to my elf. It said that I was supposed to buy gifts for her and Dad and that my budget was $2.06.

For Mama, I picked out a gold necklace that had coin-style medallions dangling off the chain. Sensing my trouble choosing a gift for Dad, the elf said that he might like a handkerchief. I wasn't going to argue with an elf who was supposed to know more than I did about what people wanted.

Once I was finished shopping, we gift wrapped the necklace and the handkerchief and taped on the gift tags and bows before leaving the secret shop. For being a good shopper, I was given a candy cane and was taken back to Mama, who sat at a table having a peaceful coffee break before being interrupted by my elf and me.

A BLAST FROM THE PAST

When PKs begin high school, our problems usually shift from the harmless variety to the criminal. Most of us are guilty by association. Some are accomplices who provide encouragement and assistance to our friends who carry out the devilish deeds.

My parents pulled the rug out from under my feet right before I started high school. We moved. I was ripped like Velcro from my childhood friends as we left one island on the southern Atlantic coast for another. We said good-bye to St. Simons Island, Georgia, and hello to Hilton Head Island, South Carolina.

For pastors who are considering moving to a new place when their kids are adolescents, I should offer a word of advice: *don't do it.* The beginning teenage years are challenging enough for normal kids, but PKs have double trouble making new friends at that stage of life.

After the decision to move, the second mistake that happened was that I was put into a private school. When we moved to Hilton Head in 1979, there was no public middle school or high school on the island. They were on the mainland, a half-hour away. A church member provided a scholarship for me to attend one of the two private schools and encouraged my parents to go that route. Mama enrolled me in Sea Pines Academy.

Cliquishness was rampant at the beginning. The church youth group had a schism that pitted the students of the private schools against each other. We had some cheerleaders and athletes from each of the schools in our church. They were the worst.

One Wednesday night, there was a fight at prayer meeting over the speed of the cheers that were performed during the basketball games. The May River Academy cheer was much slower than the Sea Pines Academy cheer, and the SPA group said it was because the MRA kids themselves were "slower." The MRA kids said that the SPA kids acted all charismatic about everything and that fans could not understand the cheers when they were said too fast.

These people made me want to go back to Georgia even more. Georgia is not a good state to leave to begin with, particularly for native Georgians, because it never stops reaching for those who love it; but I had no choice. I went from soft, fuzzy peaches to prickly, peeling palmetto bushes. The only solution I could see was moving to the public school.

Mama was the one who was most easily convinced that the public school was the right one for me. She knew that I had made only one friend between November and June and that if I was forced to side with one of the schools, I would not be making any friends at all for the right reasons. The obvious neutral turf was the middle ground of the public school.

Within a few weeks of beginning ninth grade, I had made more friends than I had made in the six months prior. One of them was Doug. He was a new kid, too, from California. But he was a livewire. A "surfer dude."

For starters, he'd cheated on a test in a way none of my friends would have ever considered. After we were given a study guide, Doug snuck back into the classroom during a lunch period when the teacher wasn't there. He taped his cheat sheet onto the ceiling above his desk. When it looked like he was holding his head back, deep in thought, he was reading what was up there.

Another prank Doug pulled was looking up girls' dresses. He laced a mirror under his shoe strings. When he struck up a conversation with a girl wearing a skirt, he slid his foot forward to get the mirror into the revealing position. One time he even won a bet with a girl about what color underwear she was wearing! She never figured out how he could tell.

As we were doing research in the library one afternoon during the lunch break, Doug thought it would be cool to see if we could make the librarian go into a panic. Mrs. Greenley was old and had a bad attitude about helping students. She'd made Doug mad on more than one occasion, and he wanted to even the score.

I didn't like his idea, but I wasn't going to try to keep him from carrying out his plan. He enlisted the help of a Vietnamese student named Trinh, who was always looking for trouble and never got caught. The two of them would set off some firecrackers in the library the following day.

The plan was to deposit them behind a row of books on a shelf by the back door of the library. They would light an extended fuse and then nonchalantly walk out the door, away from the scene.

Even though I didn't plan to take part in the blasting, I'd agreed to be in the library when the action went down. My job was to ask for help from Mrs. Greenley to divert attention. I was to report back to Doug and Trinh and tell them how she reacted. Once my papers were in place to make it look like I was in the library for academic reasons, I saw Doug give the thumbs up sign.

Mrs. Greenley was seated behind the counter, and her assistant was in her office behind the glass partition that looked out into the library. There were several other students in the library when it happened, but nobody saw Doug light the fuse that wrapped its way around the edge of the books. He and Trinh then casually exited the building.

Despite the rarity of school shootings in the early 1980s, library occupants thought that we were under fire. There wasn't a soul who did not hit the floor when the gunfire noises started. Including me. When I saw everybody else drop and cover their heads, I followed suit.

There must have been a hundred firecrackers attached to the fuse. When they finally stopped going off, everyone got up wondering if anyone was dead. One boy tried to leave the library, but Mrs. Greenley's assistant put us all under library lockdown until the assistant principal arrived for interrogations.

Mrs. Greenley looked like she'd been on a battlefield. Her hair was going every which way, and her glasses were crooked. Tears were spilling from her eyes, and she was shaking as her assistant comforted her. As I watched the two women emotionally break down, for a split second I considered turning Doug and Trinh in for the attempted murder of Mrs. Greenley because I was fearing she would have a heart attack. But I knew that no physical harm had come of the prank and that there would be grave consequences for anyone found guilty.

When Mr. Arcos burst in, he was outraged. Not knowing who was responsible, but figuring that it had to be someone in the library, he let us have it! Once he quarantined the library and separated the students by putting us each at our own table, he assumed full control and asked Mrs. Greenley's assistant to take her to the nurse. She needed to go home for the rest of the day after checking her blood pressure and pulse.

Until Mr. Arcos walked toward the shelf where the evidence lay, I hadn't thought to look at the damage. Books were blown off the shelf onto the floor, their pages in shreds and browned around the edges. Tattered firecracker hulls littered the area. Mr. Arcos got one and held it up to those of us waiting to be questioned.

"This is grounds for expulsion," he screamed. "Does anyone here have anything to say?"

Of course, no one did. Who would respond to anyone in such a rage?

The library assistant returned and was ordered to be the watchdog as Mr. Arcos questioned us one by one. I got to miss the next two classes, because I was the last student to be searched and questioned that day. Not one of the other students in the library knew anything other than what they had observed.

One student told Mr. Arcos that he suspected that the guilty party had gotten out of the library before the explosion had occurred. That was as close as Doug and Trinh came to being caught for upsetting Mrs. Greenley and potentially causing the evacuation of the entire school.

A letter went home, reassuring parents that our school was a safe place for us to learn. It would be almost two decades before the word Columbine took on a second meaning. If that same prank were carried out today, it would make national news and would not be considered a harmless prank as it was more than twenty years ago. The threat alone would be enough to convict and imprison.

In no way do I consider this particular confession a humorous one or a light one: I should have suffered serious consequences for aiding and abetting Doug and Trinh. But my choice to go along with their plan and not rat them out illustrates the lengths to which PKs will go to fit in and be part of the crowd during our adolescent years. We make some bad choices. Thank goodness I had parents I feared.

Update: In a recent Facebook search for Doug, I discovered that he returned to California and is a physician.

FIRST KISS

When preachers go on youth retreats with their adolescent offspring, they don't realize how badly they can damage the psyche of their children. Mine was damaged at the tender age of thirteen, and it hasn't been quite right since.

Youth retreats are designed to assist parents in training up a child in the way that he should go so that when he is old, he will not depart from it. Nowhere does it say that the parents should accompany the child on these sojourns, because along the path of self-discovery, somewhere there awaits a first kiss. Had I known where mine awaited, I'd have never closed my eyes.

Mama had given me the sex talk when I was ten. Dad didn't take part in the presentation. That told me that Mama knew a lot more than he did.

Somehow or another, all the stages of foreplay got omitted from the list of things to be addressed. Mama went directly from the part about how girls start their periods and become women to what we are forbidden to do until we are married because it brings forth babies. I couldn't imagine anybody wanting a baby enough to do a thing like that. Nauseating doesn't begin to describe the feeling that came over me when I thought about what my parents had done to get me.

If it hadn't been for all my friends' input, the foreplay parts would have remained a mystery until they became self-defense grounds for murder. But that's what friends are for. They instruct us on passionate kissing and other things when our parents leave those parts out.

Jeannine Godfrey said that I was supposed to feel heat first. If I didn't feel heat somewhere inside, then it wasn't okay to kiss the boy. The only time that the heat rule didn't apply was when people wanted to practice first. She had practiced with Dodd Wheeler on an agreed-practice basis so that she could get it right before it mattered with someone who gave her the heat. I declined a practice session with anyone, so Jeannine used Barbie and Ken as demo dolls.

The next thing that had to happen was the arm positioning. Jeannine said that the boy's arms had to go around the girl's waist and that the girl's arms go up around the boy's neck. This is because the boy should feel the girl's curves. Since boys are usually taller, the girl's arms around his neck help tilt the girl's head just so.

Once the heat was on, the hands were in place, and the heads were tilted, the lips could meet. Jeannine reminded me to pay close attention to this part, because things had to happen in a certain order for it to count as a real kiss. When the lips met, they had to be together at the beginning. Once the contact was made with mouths closed, the mouths would open, but the eyes would shut. There were just too many things to remember, as far as I was concerned.

Since Barbie and Ken were ineffective for the next part of the instruction, Jeannine said to pretend I had a

Jawbreaker in my mouth. I asked her if it could be an Atomic Fireball instead, and she said she thought so. I got one for each of us from my secret stash so we wouldn't have to pretend. Jeannine showed me how to lick a circle around it, and said that the Fireball would be like the boy's tongue.

My fireball shot out of my mouth like a cannon and rolled across the floor. Just the thought of somebody else's spit in my mouth made me want to hurl. I almost did.

Jeannine said she didn't think I was ready for any more information. She said that one day when I felt the heat, I'd forget all about the spit and focus on the kiss. I didn't think so, but I didn't argue. Up until then, I hadn't understood why I had to leave the room whenever my Meema Haynes watched *As the World Turns*. Now I knew.

A couple of years later, a youth group from Ringgold, Georgia, came to a retreat at our church. There were some good-looking guys in that crowd, but none cuter than Willis Ledbetter. He was tall, with brown hair, and long eyelashes that God was supposed to have given to me instead of wasting them on a boy.

For most kids, the approach would have been simple. But I was the PK in the group, and having Dad around was intimidating for boys who otherwise would have been relaxed and eager to talk. Therefore, I was the one who had to make the first move.

By the end of the weekend retreat, I had held hands with my first puppy love. Jeannine was right about the heat. When his hand had touched mine during a film in the recreation room, I melted in my chair. Both of the youth groups had enjoyed making friends. I wasn't the only one crying when the Ringgold church bus pulled out of the parking lot on its way back home.

For the next two months, Willis and I wrote letters and called each other. Our youth group had planned a reciprocal trip to Ringgold for a retreat on their turf. Willis and I would be together again soon.

At the Ringgold church, there was a recreation facility that had ping pong and pool tables upstairs, above the church kitchen. The dimly lit stairwell leading up had a landing halfway. Most of our group had already gone upstairs once we got off the bus, but I was so nervous about seeing Willis that I had to pee first.

Meanwhile, Willis headed downstairs to greet me after someone told him that I'd made a pit stop at the restroom. We met on the stairwell landing, and the heat welled up inside. It made my legs wobble. I think my heart stopped, too. Since everyone else was already upstairs, Willis and I were alone. This was the moment. My first kiss. Halfway between upstairs and downstairs on a landing in a church recreational complex.

Willis didn't follow the directions. He must not have been given his instructions yet, so I had to take the lead. Nothing was in sync. We were doing two different dances. Instead of putting his hands around my waist, his hands cupped my elbows so that I couldn't put my arms around his neck. He wasn't feeling my curves!

According to Jeannine, kissers are both supposed to tilt their heads so that their chins are slightly to their right and their foreheads slightly to their left. Willis got it backwards and our noses bumped on the approach. He forced me to tilt my head the wrong way. I was so addled that I closed my eyes before the contact.

As we kissed, I couldn't figure out how Jeannine associated this part with a Jawbreaker. It was much softer. I just kept my eyes closed and focused on following the directions. Then it was over.

When we finally made it upstairs, I hurried over to tell Jeannine that Willis and I had kissed. But this was not news to her.

Jerry Parker overheard me and said, "We know. We saw you."

"What do you mean you saw me?" I asked. "We were on the stairs by ourselves. No one else was around."

"That's what you think," Jeannine countered. "A whole group of us walked right past the two of you making out. Your dad was with us, and he is not happy."

Pranks were the name of the game in this youth group. The last really good one was when Tina Sullivan hung Teddy Perkins's underwear from a flagpole on a camping trip. I wasn't about to fall for their joke. My eyes might have been closed on the stairwell, but they were wide open to my friends' tricks.

The problem for me was that they weren't joking. I kept laughing them off whenever they taunted me. Had I taken them seriously, I might have been more prepared for Dad's confrontation when he privately pulled me aside from the group.

"I have never deliberately embarrassed you, Kim, and I'm not going to tell you that you can't have feelings for boys," he began, "but you are not ready for any kisses of a passionate nature." He said some other things, too, but after the first statement, everything else became like liquid words that made no sense because my sense of hearing went warped.

Facing the others was painful, but not as shameful as facing Dad after he'd witnessed my first feeble attempt at kissing. To this very day, as a married woman, I cannot kiss with my eyes closed. Even in the dark.

IS THIS OXFORD?

It may seem strange to think of preachers as artists, but that's exactly what they are. They are masters at saying the same thing hundreds of different ways because their sermons require repetition of key thoughts and ideas in order to drive the message home. PKs are typically good language arts students because our dads foster good grammar and vocabulary.

Though he is no creative painting or drawing artist and certainly is *not* a musical artist (even with spoons), Dad is the most creative language artist on our family tree. While Saturday nights were my soaking nights, they were Dad's whisper-reading nights. This was when he polished the sermon that he had spent the week preparing for the following Sunday morning.

The most audible sounds I heard as he reread his writing aloud were the *sh*, *s*, *sp*, and *p* sounds that can be heard best from a whisperer. At first, I thought he was rehearsing something he had memorized; later I realized that his reading aloud was his way of hearing his own words to see if they made sense and flowed meaningfully. Abraham Lincoln utilized this same technique in preparation for his speeches.

Precise word choice has always been vitally important to Dad. I suppose this is the reason that he made such lasting memories on family vacations when he let his cognitive guard down. Such a time was when my family took a two-week vacation to England.

People who spend a substantial amount of time in a place where the accent is different would probably agree that by the end of a week somewhere else, the accent is acquired. Vacationers in England return home with a temporary British accent; visitors to Tennessee go home resonating a deep Southern drawl.

Besides the language itself, foods and other cultural aspects of different places demand our utmost observation. Crumpets and biscuits are similar pieces of bread that are regarded quite differently on opposite sides of the Atlantic Ocean! When I spied two bowls of crumpets next to the tea service in the lobby of our bed and breakfast, I couldn't wait to try one.

As I was deciding whether to have white or wheat, I saw out of the corner of my eye that a woman was eyeing me suspiciously. Feeling pressured, I picked up one of each and walked back over to share one with Ken. The woman was aghast as I handed Ken a wheat crumpet and popped the white one into my mouth. Three jaws dropped: mine, Ken, and our observer's. Ken and I had bitten into lumps of white and brown sugar used to sweeten the tea.

In our Ebury Street bed and breakfast room one evening, we were exhausted from the day of museums and bookshops and the evening of theater. As our heads hit the pillow and the light was put out, the sounds on the street below became familiarly audible. We distinguished cars from buses, voices, and other recognizable noises.

But there was a sudden noise that prevailed over all others: a quickening *tap...tap...tap...tap...* that became progressively louder. In the dark silence of the room, Dad spoke to Mama in his slight British accent and phrasing. “Miriam,” he said, “I do believe I hear a drip.”

We were all hearing the drip, and we were wondering if the plumbing was a problem in this antique bed and breakfast where everyone on the same floor shared a bathroom. After further sensory observation, we determined that the drip was coming from the direction of the window. Ken popped up from his bed to investigate.

As he peered out the window at the street below, he chuckled and then explained what we'd been hearing. Dad had coined a new British term: a “drip” is a British woman walking quickly in high heels down the paved sidewalk.

On that same trip, we learned that an elevator is a “lift.” It seemed rather oxymoronic when a department store employee gave us directions that included taking the lift down to the second floor. Ken and I raised our eyebrows at each other. Lift down?

Dad coined the most enduring phrase as we traveled along the subway, or “tube,” as Londoners call it. When the train stops at a platform, passengers are reminded to “mind the gap” by paying attention to the distance between the platform and the train as they step off. It was not our turn to step off yet—in fact, it was not anybody's turn to step off—and everyone on the train knew that. Subway trains must sometimes stop underground to allow other trains to continue their passage along an intersection so that collisions are avoided.

In pitch dark silence—this time in a crowded stopped subway train—Dad stole the moment. "Is this Oxford?" he wondered aloud. The laughter that his question prompted was not limited to our family. For us, and for other passengers on the train, Oxford had become someplace more than just another subway stop; it was any place that was a confusing, dark nowhere. Finally, I had a word for describing my brother's realm.

PENS

What is it with preachers and pens, anyway? Are they all as hung up with writing utensils as my dad is? I believe so. Despite the computer revolution, the pen is still what fascinates Dad and keeps him occupied for hours on end. If it's true that the best gift a church can give its pastor's wife is the gift of time alone, then it's twice as true that the gift a pastor most appreciates is a cool pen.

There was once a clever elf who told me that my dad would like a handkerchief for Christmas. Either that particular elf was a fake or it didn't know I was choosing a gift for a preacher. I believe that it was my mother's fault for not writing "preacher" on the line beside *dad* on the Santa's Secret Shop checklist. Even an elf on crack would have led me to the pens had it known Dad's occupation.

It must be the amount of writing involved in the profession that keeps pens interesting to ministers. Apparently, smooth rolling balls and fountain tips make the work seem fun. Flairs and ballpoints are like rainy days.

Other PKs will confirm that pens can even affect moods. Give a preacher a pen that is less than satisfactory and watch what happens. Then, apologize for the mistake and produce a pen that writes so deliciously that it seems to have been touched by God himself. Try it as a science fair project and experiment with preachers of all races and religions by offering them an array of pens to sample. My hypothesis is that the results will be the same for all of them. They will all hand back the cheaper pens and even attempt to hide a few of the good pens. Don't think a preacher won't try to steal a good pen. When it comes to a good pen and a preacher, it's as if Exodus 20:15 was written in disappearing ink!

Mama wishes that Dad's pens all had disappearing ink. Every good shirt he gets, he ruins because of the pens that leak in his pockets. Edna at the dry cleaners always calls Mama when a new stain removal product comes out. I guess Edna figures that if she can get Dad's ink stains out, she can go on television with the best AD campaign a small town business has ever known. They'll probably discover a cure for cancer first.

Once I figured out that Dad liked pens so much, he got a lot of them for Christmas and birthdays. Pens that stand up in holders with feathers attached like quills. Pens that are magnetic and float like magic in the middle of a disk. Pens that play "Happy Birthday" and "O Little Town of Bethlehem." Pens that have built-in LCD date and time functions. Pens that smell like strawberries, grapes, and oranges. Pens that light up in neon colors with the push of a button. Even a few gag gift pens with naked women on them that I gave him as a joke. Mama didn't think it was funny.

Sometimes pens can cause problems. I remember a few times that I got in trouble for writing notes with them in class. Pookie Hortense used one as a weapon once when he got into a fight with Jessica Stalvey. It got him suspended for five days, and it got Jessica an Ace Bandage for a week and out of school for the rest of the day after the fight.

For people who have problems with their shoelaces getting in knots all the time, pens can undo the trouble. Maggie Bennett taught me how to use a pen to free myself from knots by sticking the point of the pen through the tight spot to wiggle it loose. She said that the prong of a fork actually works best but that at school when a fork is not always available, a pen is a good substitute since pencil leads will break every time. When Marvin Pirtle tied my shoelaces together when I was working on my math puzzle, Maggie came to my rescue after the fall. Later, I was able to put Maggie's lesson to use to help Carson Day escape from her desk when she'd tied the sash of her dress in a knot around the seat and feared that if there was a fire, she'd burn up.

Problems and solutions provided by pens are one thing. Laughter is another. We got plenty of that one Sunday morning when Dad came in late for church. Usually he was in the sanctuary before the organist began the prelude and meditation, but on one particular Sunday morning, he came flying in the side door looking at his watch, skipped a step on his way up to the podium, and explained that the construction worker who was remodeling his office in the building next to the sanctuary had him hinged in. Dad couldn't get out and had been pounding for several minutes before he phoned the nursery attendant's extension, asking for some help. Dad was able to open the door before the person arrived, however, and was finally in the pulpit.

From the beginning of his story about why he was late, the congregation had been laughing full-bellied laughs, looking at each other, with hands covering their mouths and eyebrows raised. Mama had her face buried in both hands, wishing she could crawl under the pew and slither out the door unseen. Dad thought that his experience was what had tickled the congregation's funny bones, but that wasn't what had everyone in stitches.

In his panic about being trapped in his office and running late for the service, Dad had been chewing on a pen, which is what he always does when he's nervous. The ink cartridge leaked as he chewed, causing the ink to run all over his face. By the time he got out of his office, walked over to the sanctuary, and explained his story to the waiting crowd, he looked like he'd found a blackberry pie on the way to church and had been hungry and forkless.

Fortunately for Dad, his church members have always loved him and laughed with him and not at him. Not that they ever let him live it down, but they did make the best of having an impromptu songfest until Mama could get Dad's face cleaned up so that he could return and deliver the message without looking like Bozo. Ironically, there had been five visitors from up north in church that morning. We still wonder if they shake their heads and mumble, "God, help those Southern Baptists."

CAMP LEO

Each summer on Hilton Head Island, the Lions Club sponsors Camp Leo for blind children across the state of South Carolina. Some campers are completely blind, some partially, but all legally. In order for the camp to run smoothly, volunteers are needed at all hours.

PKs who have a knack for working with children usually discover it as they help out in the church nursery and assist during Vacation Bible School. That's where I entertained my first serious thoughts of becoming a teacher. One of Mama's friends was a special education teacher who'd been trying to persuade me to consider that field. Mama clipped the article from the newspaper thinking that I might like to call the number and volunteer some of my summer afternoons.

When I arrived at camp for the first time, I had no idea what to expect. I would be working with fifth, sixth, and seventh graders doing crafts, going to the beach, and swimming. My job was to make sure that the campers remained safe and to assist with their projects and activities.

Each of the campers was special, but two of the boys made a tremendous impact on my life. Their names were Todd and John. Even though I tried not to show favoritism, I was partial to these two campers.

Todd was an African American who could make out large shapes and see light. He wore glasses to make the images sharper. Reading was possible, but difficult. Writing was sloppy but discernible.

Todd didn't consider his limited sight a deterrent to his relationships. He strutted around wearing sunglasses for the better part of the week, flirting with all the girls. Here was a boy whose self-confidence lacked nothing, who believed in himself, and radiated happiness in every direction. Who ever thought that a blind boy couldn't be a ladies' man?

John was a Filipino with smooth olive skin and black hair in a buzz cut. As Southerners would say about someone who is slightly overweight, John "carried around a little extra." When we went swimming, I had to hold him in the pool because he couldn't swim. He felt like a big, soft teddy bear.

Baths were a regular part of John's life, but he'd never been in a swimming pool before. I taught him how to hold his breath and go under the water and to blow bubbles. He held on to the side of the pool and kicked.

As I was taking him back to sit on the edge of the pool so that I could help another camper get into the water, John asked, "What is it like?"

"What?" I clarified, "The pool?" I asked, unsure of what he meant.

"No, the water. When I kicked it, what did it do?"

People don't realize how much we take for granted until we spend time with someone who has limitations that we don't have. I'd never thought about what water looks like when kicked. "Well, I guess I'd say that it goes off into tiny drops, and then the drops fall back into the rest of the water," I ventured.

"Oh. Did I make a lot of drops? Can I hold one?"

I hadn't explained that the drops of water don't remain separated when they hit the surface of the pool, so I re-explained the concept as best I could. It's hard to imagine what was going through John's mind when he'd never seen anything before. What is an image to a completely blind person who has been that way since birth?

I wasn't prepared for his next remark. With a smile on his sweet little innocent face, John dreamily said, "I sure wish I could see it, too." Being in the pool made the touching experience convenient for the tears I could not hold back.

Volunteering at camp, I thought I was there to guide and teach. Instead, I became the student, learning life lessons that couldn't be taught in any classroom. The Bible says, "a little child shall lead them," and it's true. Children do.

The years beyond camp brought occasional letters from John and Todd. John's were easy to read, because someone else wrote his. Todd's were more difficult to decipher, even though every letter he sent had a "P.S. Please excuse my sloppy writing." But one letter that came in December left me in a quandary when I read it.

At Christmastime, cards and letters pour in wishing happy holidays. Preachers get plenty of Christmas cards from their current and past church members, family, and local businesses. When our newspaper deliveryman sent one, Dad wasted no time putting a ten dollar bill in a card for him. He said that he didn't want to get another card from the same newspaper delivery man saying, "Merry Christmas" again, this time stamped in bold letters *Second Notice*.

A one dollar bill fell out when I opened the letter from Todd. After wishing my family and me a Merry Christmas, he explained that things were not so good at home. His thirty-four-year-old father had perished in an automobile accident, leaving his mother to raise four children alone. He explained that he'd wanted to get me a nice gift for Christmas but that money was tight, and so maybe I could pick something out with the dollar he'd enclosed.

If a preacher hadn't been handy in the house, I'd have sought one for immediate consultation. Part of me was shocked about the death of Todd's father. Another part of me was happy that he considered writing to me important even at a tragic time in his life. The part that I wrestled with was keeping the dollar when I knew the predicament of his family. Dad read the letter and said that he'd need a few days to think about what I should do and that he'd soon have an answer.

Every preacher's kid gets mentioned from time to time in sermons. Our behaviors and adventures are used to illustrate points—the good, the bad, and the ugly. The following Sunday morning as I sat in church, I had no idea that my answer was about to be part of Dad's sermon.

Dad prefaced the reading of a portion of the letter by giving a brief history of my relationship with Todd and a summary of what was happening in his life. He then read a portion of the letter that brought forth tears and sniffles throughout the sanctuary. After the reading, Dad explained to the congregation that he was sharing this because I had come to him seeking advice on what to do with the dollar.

From the pulpit, Dad responded directly to me. "You had no idea that your answer was coming this morning, but I believe that you should keep the dollar. It's the best gift you've ever been given, because it came from the heart of the giver in the true spirit of giving, when this young man had nothing to spare." Dad had delivered not only the advice that I needed, but also a poignant Christmas message for his parishioners.

Todd and his family moved and left no forwarding address shortly after his father's death. I still pursue trying to locate him every now and then. Perhaps he'll make it easy for me and do what John did.

Several years ago, John called to say thanks for what I'd meant to him the summer that I volunteered at Camp Leo. I told him that the feelings were mutual, but I didn't feel that I could bring up the pool story without breaking down. At the time of his phone call, he was earning a business degree from a South Carolina college. Limitations had not kept John from achieving his dreams.

May we all offer of ourselves in the true spirit of giving. For some, it's money. For others, it's time. In either case, generosity reaps rewards caboodles of times its investment.

GUTS AND GLORY

When I was in high school, a science teacher assigned a term paper. Each student in the class had a week to choose a topic. Once we'd decided, we were to confer with the teacher to get our specific topics approved.

Most of my classmates didn't need the whole week to think about it. On the other hand, a few could have had the rest of the school year and still would have remained undecided, hence the deadline. I knew my topic as soon as the teacher gave the guidelines.

An avid Steven King fan and a PK, I decided to combine my senses of morbidity and serenity. My topic was mortuary science with an emphasis on embalming. The work of a mortician requires guts and glory, and I wanted to see if I had what it took, just in case I nixed my plan to become a teacher.

For once in my life, I was glad my teacher was a man. He didn't hesitate to approve my topic. Mr. Nolan had a smirk on his face as he made a note beside my name of the list. But my friends were not as unaffected.

"What? Are you out of your mind?" they all asked with more exclamation point than question mark. But they already knew the answer, so I don't know why they bothered asking in the first place. Of course I was out of my mind. PKs have to be out of our minds in order to endure what we go through.

Mama's blank stare didn't surprise me. "Why do you want to go and do something like that?" she asked, her eyes glazed and unblinking.

"That's the strange thing, Mama," I said. "Usually it takes me awhile to decide on something. You know, like at Scoops. I go back and forth between chocolate and peppermint swirl ice cream then change my mind half a dozen times before deciding on banana. But not today; not with my topic. I didn't waver a bit."

"Well, it must run in our family," Mama wailed, covering her face with her hands. "And it runs on *my* side."

I offered to change my topic when I saw how it upset Mama so. But she wouldn't hear of it. "Let's just do this and get it over with," she sobbed, wiping her eyes with a Kleenex. "That's what your DeeDaddy Jones had to do to get it out of his system. He changed his mind quicker than a Yankee talks."

It turned out that DeeDaddy had once considered buying a funeral home in Glennville, Georgia. His plan was to work there as a custodian while attending classes to attain the required credentials to become a funeral director. Once things were in place, DeeDaddy would secure the financing and purchase the funeral home from Mr. Brown.

Less than a week later, Mr. Brown knew that the deal was off when he came in one morning and discovered the front parlor in disarray. The broom lay in the middle of the floor. A broken lamp was propped between its table and a wall. The front door had been left unlocked, and the lights were on.

DeeDaddy never told anybody what had happened. All Meema knew was that he came home from work early one night, looking like he'd seen a ghost and probably had. He slept on the couch with the lights on for five nights and wouldn't eat his eggs.

The rest of the meals Meema could justify as loss of appetite. But DeeDaddy could count on one hand the number of days in his entire life that he hadn't eaten two eggs for breakfast. After five in a row, Meema bargained with God, and DeeDaddy snapped out of his funk.

"You treat this as you would any mention of a frog around Meema," Mama told me. Frogs and toads were taboo with Meema. Those were the two things in the world that sent her into oblivion. She feared my research would, too, if she found out about it.

I arranged for an interview with Mr. Underwood of Underwood & Sons Funeral Home in Savannah, Georgia. Mama waited in the car with a book while I toured the facility. A display of caskets filled one room; others downstairs were for family viewings and memorial services. Upstairs, Mr. Underwood said, was the room where the bodies were embalmed.

As we headed in that direction, I felt a few flutters in the pit of my stomach. Most everyone eventually ends up in a room of its kind—or a crematory—but I wondered about what percentage of the population purposely wandered into one before it became necessary.

I'll admit that it was a bit creepy at first, but once I was in the room and began to understand the science of preserving a body, I felt at ease. In the middle of the room, there was a steel table that tilted to allow fluids to drain. One day, I resolved, I would see firsthand what Mr. Underwood was describing to me.

By the time I'd conducted the interview and funeral home and crematory tour, the books on the process made more sense. My research was complete. Piece by piece, my term paper came together. When we handed in our term papers on the due date, each person had to stand and give an overview of their topic and what they had learned. Jenna McCullough raised her hand and asked Mr. Nolan if he would listen to my overview one-on-one because her grandmother had recently passed away and it would be too upsetting. Also, she was afraid I'd make people sick. I agreed, and so did Mr. Nolan.

For six years, my idea of becoming a mortician lay dormant. Then, one of my college professors in the education department conducted an activity that resurrected the notion. Dr. Billings had us close our eyes and think of what we'd considered becoming if we hadn't been on our way into teaching. She encouraged us to explore our second-choice professions for two reasons: first, to rule out any second thoughts about becoming a teacher, and second, to have a backup plan in case we became teacher burnout statistics.

Later that week, I called a local funeral home and explained that I was on assignment to witness an embalming. They told me that it was not their policy to allow the general public to watch what they do, because it would violate the privacy of the individual's family. Since they had taken my name and phone number, I wasn't too surprised when Mr. Hoppe called back late that night and invited me over to the funeral home.

All two-story funeral homes must put the embalming room upstairs, probably so that no one wanders in looking for a restroom and ends up using it as one anyway. People don't wander upstairs in a mortuary without some idea of what might be up there.

When I arrived at the funeral home, Mr. Hoppe escorted me upstairs where a sixty-something-year-old heart attack victim lay on the embalming table. He was covered from his waist to his knees with a sheet, and I noted that if I hadn't known better, I'd have thought he was in a peaceful slumber and scheduled to be at work the next morning.

"So you are considering becoming one of us?" Mr. Hoppe asked. Surely he was referring to morticians in general, and not the deceased. I thought I detected a hint of smugness in his question.

I didn't want him to think that this was just a whim. "Actually, I've been thinking about it since I started high school. I've researched the profession, and it appeals to me. That's why I'm glad you called me so that I could take things one step further in my decision before I become a teacher."

"Well, you wouldn't have to shush anybody in this line of work," Mr. Hoppe noted. "Of course, from time to time we do have to tell them to be still."

"What do you mean?" I was confused. Dead people don't move around.

Mr. Hoppe took a scalpel and slit the jugular vein on the right side of the deceased's neck. Now that I'd seen a dead person not bleed, I knew that much was true. He inserted a vacuum tube and a pump tube into the vein and artery. One put preservation fluid into the body, and the other pumped the blood out.

"The first time I saw one move, it wasn't too dramatic," Mr. Hoppe explained. "The nerves sometimes cause the body to jerk a bit. If you've ever chopped the head off a snake, then you've seen what I'm talking about."

The image was bothersome, to say the least. I looked to make sure that the white sheet was motionless. I figured that Mr. Hoppe was pulling my leg.

"The worst body jerk I ever saw was when I was in school. A group of young students was in the room—myself included. I was glad I wasn't by myself, because one second the cadaver was flat on the table and the next it was sitting straight up like it was ready to eat a Big Mac. Now that was awesome," Mr. Hoppe reminisced.

My face must have indicated disbelief, because Mr. Hoppe wanted to prove that it happens. "Sometimes it seems like they can still hear us when we talk to them. I haven't tried this trick in a long time, but it usually works. You just say the man's name and tell him to lift his arm. You want to try it?"

I shook my head.

"Okay, then, I'll do it." Mr. Hoppe said the man's name and then directed him to lift his arm. Nothing happened. He tickled his foot. Nothing.

I nearly jumped out of my skin when the telephone rang on the counter across the room. Mr. Hoppe walked over to the counter to answer it. Judging from the end of the conversation I was hearing, it sounded like the deceased's widow discussing burial attire.

The entire experience seemed surreal. There I was in a mortuary watching a mortician perform his art. In the midst of trying to communicate with the dead man, the phone rang and it was the beloved wife of the deceased man. If she'd had any idea what she'd interrupted, she'd have been mortified herself.

As Mr. Hoppe continued his telephone conversation, I looked closely at the man on the table. A husband. A father? An uncle? Probably a businessman. Maybe a doctor? Whoever he was, he'd woken up that morning ready to face the day and would face no more.

I reverently studied his facial features. Suddenly, his eyebrows lifted and then fell. It wasn't my imagination. I screamed, flew down the stairs, and ran to my car. It is nothing short of a miracle that I didn't get a speeding ticket on the way back to my dorm room.

Under my covers with the light on, I was certain that I had discovered DeeDaddy's mystery. As he'd swept the floor of a viewing room that fateful night, DeeDaddy had undoubtedly become a witness to a body jerk. The difference was that he'd been completely alone and not expecting it, and I had been accompanied and left a widow wondering what in the world was going on in the background of that funeral home.

Dr. Billings helped me rule out mortuary science as a profession, but she forgot to tell me that teaching requires guts and glory of a different magnitude. Teachers scream, make haste to their cars, and tear out of the parking lot at times, too. And if Mr. Hoppe ever pays me a visit in my classroom, I won't hesitate to show him why.

MIRACLES

We've all had brushes with death whether we are PKs or not. For some, disease or illness threatens. For others, accidents happen. *What if?* is a big question, with only two little tiny words, that can drive us into the ground if we don't suppress our memories of the moments that could have been our last.

God sometimes allows events to affect all of our lives for reasons that we'll never know. As we mature, sometimes we gain a different perspective on what happened. We can look back with more focused eyes and see how we became stronger as a result of our jarring experiences.

What happened to me has happened to scores of other people, through no fault of our own. We were in the right place at the wrong time when drunk drivers did what they do best. Wrecked.

I was thirteen years old, waiting on the school bus in front of the First Presbyterian Church on a crisp October morning. I attended Glynn Middle School in Brunswick, which was right across the bridge to St. Simons. Usually, four other people waited with me at our bus stop. We would put our books down and talk as we looked down King's Way for the bus to appear.

At first, I thought I'd missed the bus. The others weren't at the bus stop, and I was a few minutes late arriving. I decided to give it a few more minutes before walking back home to get a ride. Growing impatient, I kept looking back over my shoulder to see if anyone else was coming along to ride the bus that morning.

I survived the accident for one reason: God was watching over me. As I was looking back, hoping for a fellow bus rider to show up, a white car was stopped at a stop sign, about to make a right turn. The elderly woman looked back to make sure nothing was coming and then pulled out into her lane.

But a green car was passing in the intersection, and when the white car pulled out onto the main road, the green car swerved and began careening out of control, coming directly toward me. Instinctively, I ran into the churchyard, away from the road.

Running at top speed, still holding my books, I got a slow-motion feeling like in that dream where you're running down a hall that keeps getting longer as you keep running harder but keep getting slower. It was inevitable that the car would hit me. My objective was to survive with the least amount of bodily damage.

Miraculously, I did. The driver's side front fender struck the inside of my right leg, knocking me to the ground. I didn't have time to look at my injuries before I heard the glass shatter and the metal crunch. The car had spun sideways and smacked two pine trees, buckling the driver's side of the car.

I felt the searing pain in my leg, so I knew it was still attached. In fact, when I looked to see how bad it was, it didn't look broken to me. It wasn't bleeding, either.

When I looked up, two black angels were running over to see about me. I could tell that they were grandmothers, because they were soft and they smelled so good I wanted to bury my head right on the pillows of their chest and just breathe them all in. Those angels were attempting to shield me from the sight of the smashed-up car and its contents. From the looks of it, no one could have survived.

That's why it scared the bejesus out of me when the driver's door popped open and a man emerged. I thought he would surely start spiraling his way upward to heaven—or downward to hell—but he didn't. He just stumbled around the churchyard holding his head in his hands. He was bloody, but all of his extremities were intact.

By that time, cars were stopping, and people were congregating at the scene. Uncertainty and fear were likely what prompted the grandmothers to pick me up and take me to their car to wait for the ambulance. I wanted to get my school books and my purse to take with me, but I didn't see them anywhere.

When the ambulance got there, the emergency workers swarmed me with questions, strapped me onto a stretcher, and slid me into the back of the ambulance like a casserole going into an oven. I wanted to stay with the soft, black grandmothers. They didn't ask me all sorts of questions, and they weren't all panicky. I never knew who they were, but I loved them.

God sends His messengers on missions, and He appointed a faithful church member to break the news to my parents. When Mama opened the door, he said, "Kim is okay," before explaining what had happened.

He brought my parents to me. I was glad he had done the Lord's work in time for Mama to ride in the ambulance with me. The drunk driver was in there, too. Mama deserves a lot of credit for not finishing him off on the way to the hospital.

The doctor said that other than a bad bruise, I would be okay. He gave me a pair of crutches to use, but I was able to walk around without them just fine. But because the crutches helped heighten the dramatic effect of the accident, I used them for a couple of days.

When the police came to the parsonage later that evening, I realized how close I'd come to being killed. The purse I'd had on my shoulder when the car hit me had been found on the other side of the church yard. In it, I had packed a boiled egg in a sandwich bag for lunch. The eggshell had softened on impact, making it appear that I had peeled the egg before putting it in the bag. I hadn't. A mangled safety pin made mama cry.

For Mama, the what-ifs were relentless. What if Kim hadn't run? *She'd have been pinned between the car and the tree, severed in half.* What if she'd run the other way? *She'd have run into the road only to be hit by another car.* What if she hadn't run fast enough? *She'd have been found in a heap on the other side of the church yard, mangled like the safety pin, with her purse and egg.* What if the other students had been waiting on the bus that day? *There would have been fatalities for sure.*

Several days later, when the drunk driver was released from the hospital, he paid us a visit to apologize for nearly killing me. He was bandaged and stitched, looking like he'd lost a pitchfork fight with the devil. But he came bearing a gift for me, so I was pretty quick to forgive. Not many kids my age would have cared much for a book with a collection of Peanuts cartoons, but Snoopy was my second-favorite cartoon dog (I liked Scooby-Doo better), and preacher's kids grow up so poor that even a new book excites us. Mama told me to take my book in my room so that the adults could have a chat. I knew what that meant. Somebody was fixing to be eaten alive.

From what I was told after the visit, the wreck was the turning point for the man who'd hit me. This was supposed to make me feel better. He'd finally admitted that he was an alcoholic and needed to get help. Dad magnanimously forgave the man and saw that he got the support resources he needed to kick his habit. He enlisted a pastor of another church to oversee the religious counseling, since he didn't want to have to see the man's face in his congregation every Sunday.

I'm not sure Mama ever forgave him, but she didn't kill him in the ambulance either. As I see it, a drunk driver got pardoned twice that week.

GOING PLACES

As difficult as it may have been for Dad to accept the pure rottenness of some sinners, he was not naïve to the problems of the world. Waycross was just a more wholesome place to grow up without a lot of riff-raff. Granddaddy Haynes preached there for many years while he worked toward retirement from Atlantic Coast Lines Railways. His wasn't the kind of town that needed a full time preacher back in those days.

Dad's family didn't go on any vacations while he was growing up, so one thing he wanted to do for his parents was take them on a trip. When he began working on his doctoral degree from New Orleans Baptist Theological Seminary, his schooling required him to travel there several times over the course of his two year program. A vacation to New Orleans made economic sense.

We borrowed a luggage carrier from somebody in our church so that Ken and I didn't have to be crammed into the back of the station wagon with the suitcases all the way to Louisiana. Meema and Granddaddy were in the middle where Ken and I usually sat. Mama laid the rear seats flat, threw in a quilt, and put our pillows back there so that Ken and I could lie down and sleep as much as possible.

Seatbelt laws were years away, but Granddaddy always wore his. He'd officiated at so many funerals brought on by what he suspected was the lack of seatbelt usage. Future studies would prove him correct. In this respect, he was years ahead of his time. When Meema challenged him, claiming that seatbelts could also lock up and prevent people from being able to escape the wreckage, Granddaddy took to carrying a razor blade in the fold of his sock. This way, he reasoned, he could always cut himself loose if he got hung up in the seatbelt.

In other respects, Granddaddy was not exactly up to snuff. Before we went exploring in the French Quarter, Dad went over some ground rules as a safety precaution. I didn't realize it at the time, but that safety session was as much for his parents as it was for his children. Ken and I would need to hold a grownup's hand in some places. If we passed bars that had the doors open and music playing, we were not allowed to look inside. Talking to strangers was strictly forbidden. Under no circumstances were we to accept anything from anybody.

Our walk through the French Quarter and the market area was enlightening for Meema and Granddaddy, who'd never been out of the state of Georgia except to attend Dad's seminary graduation in Kentucky. Meema refused to believe that voodoo priests were real. She flat out told a tour guide, "I don't believe in all that monkey business. There's no such thing as magic."

Strip joints existed only in the imagination in Waycross, Georgia. Our clan didn't see any voodoo priests on Bourbon Street, but there was no denying the reality that women took off their clothes and danced. I might not have believed it if I hadn't broken the rule about looking into one of those forbidden bars with the music. Sure enough, there was a naked woman with a feather boa around her neck, dancing next to a pole. Dad hurried us all past that spot, because the crowd was cheering in the street and he didn't want to give pickpockets any easy opportunities.

The French Quarter was stock full of drunks. I'd seen a few drunk people before at wedding receptions and parties but nothing like what I saw sitting up against the buildings and sprawled out on the sidewalks. I'd have plenty to tell my friends. They probably wouldn't believe me.

As we trudged on down Bourbon Street, Meema spotted a man vomiting on the other side of the street. "Felix! That man over there is sick. We need to get him some help. Everybody else is just walking past the poor fellow!"

Meema was holding my hand, and Dad drew close to her and explained that the man was indeed sick, but the disease was alcoholism and it was up to the man to help himself.

"Is that right?" Meema asked, shaking her head in disbelief yet again.

When we were ready to move on, we couldn't find Granddaddy. He'd disappeared somewhere, and Dad had to go back and look for him. He didn't want to leave us alone on Bourbon Street, so he took us backtracking with him.

Dad spotted him with a busty brunette wearing a Santa suit that would have appalled Mrs. Claus. She had my granddaddy pulled to the side and was offering him a red lollipop. Dad walked up, grabbed Granddaddy by the arm, and led him away from the woman.

"Sir," the woman protested to my Dad, who ignored her and kept walking, "we were just having a chat."

When we got out of earshot, Dad scolded his father for talking to a hooker. Meema caught her breath so hard I thought she was going to pass out right there on Bourbon Street with the winos. Granddaddy got upset with Dad for making an allegation like that. He said that the young woman had just finished saying said she needed to be saved. The two were about to find a quiet spot and pray so that she could invite Jesus into her heart and ask forgiveness for her sins so that she might live forever. And besides, Granddaddy reminded Dad, if anybody posed any threat at all, he was armed with his razorblade.

From the look on Dad's face, it was clear that he wasn't going to win an argument with Granddaddy. Dad made haste in getting all of us back to the car. When we got back to our motel, there was a message.

Dad seemed all too sad to have to tell us that a church member had died and that we would have to cut our vacation short. I could have been wrong for questioning it, but all the way home I wondered whether there was really going to be a funeral or whether Dad was trying to avoid the need for a few.

THE GIFT OF TIME

One of the best gifts that a church can give a minister's wife is time alone. She needs peace and quiet, away from her husband and PKs, if she is to be good glue. No one has a more testing job. Not a doctor, not a teacher, and not an air-traffic controller. The only way that a minister's wife can hold it together and keep from becoming a serial killer on the loose is to disassociate at least a couple of times a week.

Mama's friends on St. Simons probably caught a glimpse of the killer instinct in her, but not one of them could bear the thought of babysitting the PKs while Mama took a little time for herself. I think that's why her circle of friends chipped in and organized a church drive to hire Ophelia to do it. The truth be known, Ophelia was probably the only other woman brazen enough to deal with Ken and me on a regular basis. In fact, Mama's circle also threw in a little extra for some light housekeeping chores, too. That's a testament to the able-bodiedness and firm-mindedness of Ophelia.

Every Tuesday and Thursday morning, Mama was the queen of the castle. Only she didn't stay in the castle. She went out into the kingdom alone and left her little prince and princess behind. Sometimes she went shopping. Other times she'd go have her hair fixed. A few times, she spent the entire morning in the peacefulness of the library doing nothing but reading magazines.

Ophelia was one of a vanishing breed. Too wonderful for words is what she was, and it's a shame that Ken and I are among the last generation who will ever have know the wonder and goodness of the relationship we shared with our black nanny. She put the fear of God in us and healed us when Dr. Lupee's medical science failed.

I think the world would be a better place if all children had nannies of a different race. It sure taught me to respect my black peers and their families. Ken and I learned something about Ophelia's culture, too, though hers may have been uniquely her own.

When I was sick with a stomach bug, Ophelia put peppermint and red wine in my chicken soup and lit a candle beside my bed. She served me hot tea in a cup from which she'd chipped a fresh notch along the rim. She made me drink from the notch, and she waved her hands over me as I ingested the liquid. At first, I thought she was trying to poison me, but I'll admit that I felt much better afterward.

People would say it isn't possible, and I'd be one of them if I hadn't seen it myself, but Mama sneezed one of her adenoids right out of her nose when she was getting ready to leave one Tuesday morning. She came running into the kitchen from her bathroom wearing nothing but her bra, panties, hose, and a slip, screaming and holding a Kleenex out with the adenoid prominently displayed for Ken, Ophelia, and me to see the evidence. Horror was all that we felt in that moment, until Ophelia stepped in with her ever-knowing sense of what should be done right away to rectify the problem.

"Chile, you done sneezed up yo' AD'noyd! That mean the othe'n need proteckin' so it don' fall out yo' head, cause they ward off the Spirits, don't you know," Ophelia instructed.

Half-crying, half-terrorized, Mama stood there trembling in her undergarments. Completely at Ophelia's mercy, she looked from Ken to me and then back at Ophelia with a sense of desperation I'd never seen in her before.

Grabbing a glass from the kitchen cabinet and Mama's hand, Ophelia herded us from the kitchen into the bathroom and retrieved a pair of nail clippers from the drawer. Climbing into the tub and out of the way, Ken and I watched as Ophelia plopped the toilet lid down, sat Mama on the seat, and helped her pull off her hose. She clipped off a piece of each of Mama's big toe nails and put them into the glass and then turned to me.

"Toss me that razor," she said, pointing to the corner of the tub directly behind my head.

I handed her the razor, and she told Mama to stare straight down at the floor, chin on her chest. When Mama's head was bent, Ophelia gently shaved a cusp of hair from the nape of Mama's neck and sprinkled it into the glass along with the pieces of toenail. Then, she filled the glass with water. Ophelia turned out the light and started chanting in a foreign language. We had no idea that our nanny was bilingual.

"Drink," she prescribed, handing the glass to my mother.

Mama wasn't the type to argue in the midst of a crisis. She believed in the healing powers of Ophelia's culture, and she drank every drop of water in that glass—hair, toenails, and all. To this day, that other adenoid has never come out of Mama's head. It is still hanging on in there, keeping the evil spirits at bay.

One problem for which Ophelia never found a successful cure was Ken's bedwetting. There wasn't enough Tide to tame the smell of urine in his sheets, but Ophelia suffered through his linens like a trooper, every time she came to keep us. Because she wasn't there at night, she couldn't try a lot of the nighttime remedies that her friends and relatives had used on her family bed wetters, but she did suggest the cornhusk and horsehair blessing.

Standing in the doorway of Ken's bedroom, Ophelia pounded seven nails into the wood overhead. From each nail, she hung a braided piece of horsehair, tied up with cornhusk bows at the bottom and top. For the next two weeks, the horsehair braid that was dead center in the row of seven had to touch Ken's nose every time he entered or exited the room. On day fourteen, there would be dry nights from then on. But on day fourteen, all we had was the memory of two weeks of horsehair and cornhusk blessings and the good intentions of Ophelia.

Two devastating things happened shortly thereafter that caused Ophelia to quit coming to keep Ken and me. I believe that the first thing—which was my fault—was the main reason. But Mama insists it was the second.

As tough as Ophelia was, the one thing that got to her was snakes. Snakes never gave me the heebie-jeebies like they did some people. As long as the head wasn't triangular and there was no red touching yellow, I'd handle it by putting my foot on its head and getting it by the neck. Sometimes I was bold enough to kiss it on the top of the head if I was trying to show off in front of somebody.

Mama gave me two rules when dealing with amphibians and reptiles: one, do not talk about or handle toads or frogs around Meema Jones; and two, do not mention or handle snakes around Ophelia. But Ophelia had made me mad because she had the power to spank and had used it on me. When I got mad, I didn't always follow the rules. So I broke rule number two.

In our backyard, there was an oval of monkey grass around two pine trees. From our sliding glass door, I pretended to see a snake crawl all the way from the monkey grass, up our back steps, through the crack in the sliding glass door, and into our living room somewhere. I thought that it had disappeared under the sofa, but I couldn't be sure. Since Ophelia had no cure for snakes except getting Ken and me and sitting in the middle of the dining room table until Mama got home, that's what she did.

One look at the three of us sitting in the middle of the table was all it took for Mama to reach up on top of the refrigerator and get the fly swatter after me. She must have chased me around the house for five minutes before she was satisfied with the swatting and handed the swatter over to Ophelia to finish the job to her own satisfaction yet again. It was the last spanking Ophelia would ever give me and the last time she ever set foot in our house.

That weekend, Ophelia's son, her only child, was shot and killed in a bar that sat no more than a hundred feet from the house he shared with his mother. He was a good boy—stayed close to home and hung out with the neighborhood group. Some thugs from another town ventured in, and Ophelia's son had gotten caught in the crossfire. It was a tragedy of the worst imaginable kind.

Mama said that she and Dad were the only white people at the funeral and that Ophelia asked them to sit with her and treated them like family. I like to think of us that way, still. Ophelia has since gone on to be with the Lord and her son, but in all the years since she left us, I hope that at some point she forgave me for lying to her about the snake, even though I never asked forgiveness. One day, we'll have forever to talk things over.

IT IS FINISHED

When I left for college, Dad got a prescription for medication that would enable him and Mama to finish raising my brother Ken without me there. He actually got the prescription filled. Ken blames it on me for leaving, saying that Dad missed me so much that he couldn't get a grip for a while. Mama said she would not offer up her opinion either way, because the main thing is that he is okay now. Dad is a survivor and always has been. But I find it interesting that once Ken left to make his way in the world, Dad was able to go off his medication for good. Unlike our cousin Willorene, Dad discovered that he was well after all.

Logic is my reason for being a prescription holder. Dad was affected by a touch of depression, and they say it's hereditary. I'm not blaming anyone, but the record speaks for itself on his side of the family tree. If preventative medicine is the name of the game in wellness, then a low dose might just keep me from going over the edge or out the window. I've heard that depression can creep up unannounced. If taking medication myself means that I can deal with other people without coming unglued, then I can truthfully claim that I take medication to deal with other people's problems. Things that would otherwise blow me out of the water slide right off my shoulder when I take my pill.

Besides, there is no stigma second to that of a PK. What have I got to lose?

Being raised a PK is not a *sho nuff* death sentence. In fact, it's the opposite for one hundred percent of the PKs I've ever known. We all walk by faith and eventually profess that faith to God. By doing this, we are assured that we've received a *life sentence* instead: we'll live forever in heaven. Our dads remind us of that truth every Sunday, along with the rest of the congregation. Probably, though, the rest of the congregation doesn't sense that the PKs are being more powerfully reminded, as if our trip through the pearly gates might happen sooner than anticipated if we don't pull ourselves together.

Whatever our denomination, and wherever our homes, all PKs owe a lifetime of thanks to our parents. For better or for worse, life isn't the same—for our parents or for us—once we're out of the parsonage. It is finished. Our time there is done, and whether we're turning cartwheels and jumping for joy or taking antidepressants prescribed by our therapists to help us deal with the realities of life once we are no longer living under the roofs of our childhood, one thing is for certain: our parents are patting themselves on their backs, congratulating each other on the success of our survival—and theirs—in such hostile environments.

Can a PK ever turn out normal? I asked this of a missionary's wife once, and here is her answer to me: "No. You will never be ordinary. You are extraordinary, and don't you ever forget it." Hers is an answer that gives a powerful life-changing perspective of being a little different from all the rest. I hope that every PK hears these words and ponders what they really mean. We are not cursed; we are truly blessed! Even Ken, who, despite all odds, turned out just a smidgeon on the bizarre side of "normal" but who is an extraordinary PK and brother!